PRE-SALE COPY

LESSONS IN LEADERSHIP
from the
SAINTS

*Called to Holiness,
Called to Lead*

BJ Gonzalvo, Ph.D.

WESTBOW
PRESS®
A DIVISION OF THOMAS NELSON
& ZONDERVAN

Copyright © 2017 BJ Gonzalvo, Ph.D..

All rights reserved. No part of this book may be used or reproduced by any means, graphic, electronic, or mechanical, including photocopying, recording, taping or by any information storage retrieval system without the written permission of the author except in the case of brief quotations embodied in critical articles and reviews.

Scriptures taken from the Holy Bible, New International Version®, NIV®. Copyright © 1973, 1978, 1984, 2011 by Biblica, Inc.™ Used by permission of Zondervan. All rights reserved worldwide. www.zondervan.com The "NIV" and "New International Version" are trademarks registered in the United States Patent and Trademark Office by Biblica, Inc.™

This book is a work of non-fiction. Unless otherwise noted, the author and the publisher make no explicit guarantees as to the accuracy of the information contained in this book and in some cases, names of people and places have been altered to protect their privacy.

WestBow Press books may be ordered through booksellers or by contacting:

WestBow Press
A Division of Thomas Nelson & Zondervan
1663 Liberty Drive
Bloomington, IN 47403
www.westbowpress.com
1 (866) 928-1240

Because of the dynamic nature of the Internet, any web addresses or links contained in this book may have changed since publication and may no longer be valid. The views expressed in this work are solely those of the author and do not necessarily reflect the views of the publisher, and the publisher hereby disclaims any responsibility for them.

Any people depicted in stock imagery provided by Thinkstock are models, and such images are being used for illustrative purposes only. Certain stock imagery © Thinkstock.

ISBN: 978-1-5127-8835-8 (sc)
ISBN: 978-1-5127-8836-5 (hc)
ISBN: 978-1-5127-8834-1 (e)

Library of Congress Control Number: 2017907951

Print information available on the last page.

WestBow Press rev. date: 07/05/2017

*Lord Jesus, as God's Spirit came down and
rested upon You, may the same Spirit rest
upon us, bestowing His sevenfold gifts.
First, grant us the gift of understanding, by
which Your precepts may enlighten our minds.
Second, grant us counsel, by which we may follow
in Your footsteps on the path of righteousness.
Third, grant us courage, by which we
may ward off the enemy's attacks.
Fourth, grant us knowledge, by which
we can distinguish good from evil.
Fifth, grant us piety, by which we may
acquire compassionate hearts.
Sixth, grant us fear, by which we may draw
back from evil and submit to what is good.
Seventh, grant us wisdom, that we may taste
fully the life-giving sweetness of Your love.*

—Saint Bonaventure

CONTENTS

The Calling 1

Saintliness and Leadership 39

Changing Our View of Leadership 58

Like the Saints 69

Leadership through the Years 86

Times Are Changing 120

Becoming a Leader, Becoming a Saint 142

Pray and Act 211

Suggestions for Further Readings 233

Dedication 245

Acknowledgments 247

THE CALLING

"Who among you wants to be a leader?" This was the question the speaker asked his audience as he started his presentation. I was in that audience, trying to sit still and pretending to contemplate the question. I watched out of the corner of my eye to see if any hands might go up, trying to gauge if I should raise my hand or keep still. I could have gone either way. I could have raised my hand because I believed I wanted to be a leader or that I should try to be a leader. But the uncertainty of where the speaker was going with that question left me motionless. Plus, I wanted to make sure that if I raised my hand, I would not be in the minority and risk the possibility of getting put on the spot. Well, eventually, very few hands were raised in the air; some went up with certainty while others went up with obvious hesitation.

Having participated in many leadership training activities and talks, this was not the only time I heard a speaker ask the audience this question. And on each occasion, the results were similar. It was as if the speaker knew the outcome beforehand. A few individuals would raise their hands, but clearly with hesitation. Only one to two individuals would raise their hands with apparent certainty or vigor. But much of the audience sat still like statues with hands not budging. I think many in the audience who kept their hands down were either unsure of what the question entailed or perhaps, like me, were uncertain of the consequence and embarrassed to put themselves forward. Part of me felt that if I raised my hand, I would be one of the very few doing so. I feared that the gesture might expose me to the judgment of others as being overly confident in my ability to become a leader. Plus, if I was one of the few hands to go up, there was also that potential to get asked follow-up questions and be put on the spot. There were too many possibilities and consequences for my brain to process within a span of only a few seconds, and so the safest bet was just to go with the majority, keep my hand down, and let that moment pass. I just knew deep inside that my nonresponse did not mean that I was ignoring the question at all; I was, in fact, thinking deeply about it. I just did not have enough time to process the implications of the question and my potential response. About 50 percent of me tried to convince my arm muscles to go up, but somewhere along that cognition process, I seemed to have discovered that I have preconceived thinking that leadership should come to the individual rather than be pursued. Raising my hand would make it seem as if I was intent on pursuing leadership. I could have come up with a reasonable justification to raise my hand, but given only a few seconds to process that question, keeping my hand down was the result of that internal dialogue where the active pursuit of leadership lost.

Oh well. It was a short three-second window, and it was much less strenuous for me to just sit still and keep both hands down until the speaker was done making his point. All I knew was that the real, authentic me wanted to be some kind of a leader. I just had not convinced myself enough to raise my hand and to share that with everyone else at that time. Plus, there is a fine line between confidence and arrogance, and it was a line that I did not want to have to negotiate just to be able to respond to a speaker's opening line.

Nonetheless, I have to say that I was quite fascinated by this quick little survey, and it stuck with me. It certainly piqued my interest and got me thinking. My curiosity with this phenomenon led me to wonder the same thing about another interesting domain—saintliness. I wonder if we have that same quiet ambition to be a saint as we do to be a leader. And so now, whenever I get a chance to ask a captive audience, especially when I speak at church group gatherings or teach Sunday school, I ask that same question: "Who here in the audience wants to be a saint?" And when I do get to ask that question, the response rate is strikingly similar to the leadership query—except, this time, even fewer hands go up. Apparently, few people want to be leaders, but even fewer people want to be saints.

For me, even though I hesitated to raise my hand when asked if I want to be a leader or a saint, my answer deep inside was a resounding *yes*! It may not have manifested physically but my heart was silently screaming, *Yes, I want to be a saint!* And if becoming a saint entails leadership, then, *yes*, I want to be a leader!

Perhaps it was my upbringing. I come from a collectivistic culture where you don't want to stick out like a sore thumb. I was brought up in a culture that emphasizes that actions speak louder than words and that modesty and humility must always be practiced. I must have heard my grandma's voice in my head reminding me about those virtues. I was afraid that raising my hand, especially when done casually and hastily in response to a speaker's opening line, is just a simplistic, external gesture with no intended follow-through. And who knows—maybe the audience felt the same way as I did, hence the reason for the low response rates to that question.

But I refuse to believe that very few people really want to be leaders and saints. So perhaps one underlying reason for the low response rates, including my hesitation to raise my hand, is that these are roles that we tend to think are improbable for us or even impossible for many of us. Perhaps we think that these are roles reserved only for the extraordinary and the elite—or maybe even for the otherworldly. They seem to be very ambitious roles, and I think many of us are too bashful to admit to them as something that we would like to pursue. We might think that the ambitions to become a saint or a leader are comparable to that time of naiveté when we were six years old and we told our parents that we wanted to become doctors or astronauts. Some of us might think that it is too contrived for us to desire to be a leader or a saint. Whatever our external response to these two questions, and whether we vocally say yes or raise our hands, our genuine internal response is something worth pondering because it can have implications both in the interior and exterior aspects of our lives.

Saint Therese of Lisieux, also known as the Little Flower, expressed so innocently and humbly that she desired to be a saint. Her entire brief life was devoted to the pursuit of sacrificing her preferences for the sake of the Lord's will. Even as a child, she lived her life fully intent on achieving sanctity. She really wanted to be a saint, and she made sure that she expressed it. It might sound contrived and simplistic to us, but her childhood desires became her reality. She pursued and lived out her desires, and there is no arguing with the results. She is now a canonized saint, and she stands as one of the most revered and most popular saints we have in history. She now gets to blissfully enjoy the fruits of her childlike efforts in heaven.

That same calling Saint Therese heard is ours too. It is a calling not just for the naive or the contrived or for the elite and the chosen few. We—every single one of us—are also beckoned. If we Christians, as followers of Christ, just open our hearts and minds, as Saint Therese did, then we will hear that same call to holiness.

Inherent in the call to holiness, if we just listen closely, is the call to lead. In our calling as Christians, we are called to lead one another, to empower one another, and to bring out the best in one another. It is a call within a call. Part of our response to the call to holiness is the call to be responsible for one another. One of the most influential leadership gurus, John C. Maxwell, put it this way: "A leader is one who knows the way, goes the way, and shows the way." As Christians called to follow Christ, we are called to know the way because He has shown us *the way*, along with *the truth* and *the life* (see John 14:6). As Christians in imitation of Christ, we are called not only to go *the way*, but to lead our brothers and sisters so that we may show them *the way*.

> *I must distinguish carefully between two aspects of the role the Lord has given me, a role that demands a rigorous accountability, a role based on the Lord's greatness rather than on my own merit. The first aspect is that I am a Christian; the second, that I am a leader. I am a Christian for my own sake, whereas I am a leader for your sake; the fact that I am a Christian is to my own advantage, but I am a leader for your advantage.*
>
> —Saint Augustine

Getting to Know that Someone on the Pedestal

Being a leader and being a saint are two of the most intimidating and ambitious roles we could ever aspire to in life. Both are roles that seem to be so exalted, beyond the reach of ordinary people, and reserved for those few chosen individuals. We tend to shy away from following the leadership examples of Saint Ignatius, Mother Teresa, and John Paul II, since their ability to lead and inspire others to holiness is a goal that seems to be beyond us.

Much of what the saints faced was not easy. Their perseverance and grit are to be admired. It is absolutely not my intention to minimize them one iota. But I do want to point out a hazard we can subconsciously fall into when we put the saints on a pedestal. Without giving it much thought and without delving deeper to get to know them better, many of us ordinary folks look at the saints on the pedestal and get intimidated by the thought of becoming one. We become overwhelmed and paralyzed, rendering us unable to respond to our own callings to do great things for God. Without further exploring who the saints actually were, we memorialize them, their deeds, and their moments of perfect piety. We have carved them into statues and illuminated them in paintings. We honor them with great reverence. We have raised them to places of honor, as is their due. But in so doing, we might be inadvertently dismissing the saints and ignoring their humanity too quickly.

Dorothy Day, who founded the Catholic Worker Movement in the 1930s in New York City, notably said, "Don't call me a saint … I don't want to be dismissed that easily."

Perhaps, just as Dorothy Day suspected, we fail to take the moment to look beyond the statues and the stained-glass images. We think that the call to be a saint is only for special, not-fully-human people. We think that it is not a call meant for us. But when we focus on their memorialized moments of achievements, we miss the process of how they came to be. Too often, when we see the saints memorialized on their pedestal, we fail to see the race they ran. With our limited imaginations, we fail to see the struggles and the moments of imperfections that they had to go through. We tend to think that their greatness and their saintliness were something that they were born with. We are likely to assume that they have some fixed traits that they were just naturally gifted with, or perhaps assume that they just happened to be in extraordinary circumstances that enabled them to become saints.

Our memorializing of the saints reminds us that we too have the same calling to holiness. We need to remind ourselves that the saints are inviting us on the same path to oneness with God. Dorothy Day, even though she said she did not want to be called a saint, knew that her calling was to be a saint. She wrote, "We are all called to be saints." The saints are inviting us to get to know them and inviting us to look at the details of their lives. Many of us often spend our conversations with the saints talking about ourselves, asking them for their intercessions, and asking them to pray for our personal intentions. Perhaps we should instead take the opportunity to open our ears and hearts and hear the details of their stories and of how they came to be saints. If only we try and get to know them better, we might learn that the call to becoming a saint is open and accessible to us all, to even the worst of all sinners. We will learn that the saints too were just as ordinary, as imperfect, and even as sinful as anyone of us, but they eventually persevered and chose to do the will of God.

We must get to know the saints, for it is in the details of their lives where we will find the roadmap to lead us to God. Saint Augustine's book, *Confessions,* was my first encounter with a spiritual book as a curious young adult. Saint Augustine was the very first saint I got to know deeply, and it all began with a simple accidental reading. I was not much of a reader prior to reading Saint Augustine but one day, I happened to be hanging out at one of those big-box bookstores. This was in the late 1990s, and hanging out in such bookstores was the trendy thing to do. I got my cup of coffee and started browsing around the bookstore with no real intention of reading. But as I walked around the bookstore to browse, this one book caught my eye. It had a catchy one-word title, *Confessions,* and out of curiosity, I stopped and picked it up. I read the back cover, got more intrigued, turned it, and opened to the first page. And little did I know that as soon as I read the opening lines, I would be hooked. I grabbed a seat at the café and ordered a cup of coffee for I knew that I was going to be a while. It felt as if Saint Augustine had leapt out of the pages and into the seat across the table to have a cup of coffee with me and tell me his story. It was as if he was really there to talk to me about his childhood in Thagaste and in Carthage, about his mother, Saint Monica, about his encounter with the philosophy of Manicheism, his promiscuous lifestyle, and about the other juicy details of his life.

Perhaps this ordinary hang out with some casual reading was no accident, because this moment with Saint Augustine is what I mark as the beginning of my spiritual journey. Reading about his journey got me thinking about my own. And the deeper I dove into the life of Saint Augustine through this book and his other writings, the farther I was driven into my own road of spiritual conversion. It was as if I was reading about my own search for life's meaning and for what God wants me to do in my life.

> Great art thou, O Lord, and greatly to be praised; great is Thy power, and infinite is Thy wisdom. And man desires to praise Thee, for He is a part of Thy creation; he bears his mortality about with him and carries the evidence of his sin and the proof that Thou dost resist the proud. Still he desires to praise Thee, this man who is only a small part of Thy creation. Thou hast prompted him, that he should delight to praise Thee, for Thou hast made us for Thyself and restless is our heart until it comes to rest in Thee.
>
> —Saint Augustine

Prior to my encounter with Saint Augustine's book, I was not much of a reader. I was not even a spiritual or religious person at all, for that matter. But there was something about Saint Augustine's writings that got me reading line after line and page after page. He got me hooked, and I just could not put his book down. It was a transformative moment for me in so many ways—spiritually, intellectually, holistically. I had no idea that a book could have such an effect on a person. The philosophical thoughts and words of Saint Augustine opened my eyes, my mind, and my heart.

I don't think I'm the only one who has experienced feeling this way upon reading Saint Augustine. His writings can pump spiritual fuel into any reader's life. *Confessions* is a book that not only introduces you to Saint Augustine but urges you to pursue the spiritual life and deepen your own relationship with God. Reading Saint Augustine's book helped me realize that God, in all His greatness, has made me—ordinary, little me, and sinful me—for Himself, and that my heart is truly restless until it can find rest in Him.

I felt like a whole new person after reading Saint Augustine's *Confessions*. It led me to pursue a different path in life. And with my rejuvenated interest in the pursuit of knowing more about my Creator and His wonderful creations, I eventually decided to go back to school to finish my undergraduate studies. There was something about Saint Augustine that kept drawing me to the study of philosophy and psychology. Philosophy—the love of wisdom. Indeed, I fell in love with wisdom. I don't think that it was love of wisdom for the sake of wisdom but for the sake of knowing God, our all-knowing and all-powerful God. Psychology—the study of the soul. Indeed, I wanted to know more about the human soul. Reading Saint Augustine made me recognize that my soul was thirsty for spiritual knowledge. And as I yearned to learn more about our Creator and His creations, I just kept following the trail of the pursuit of wisdom. That trail eventually led me to pursue advanced studies in the field of psychology. My curiosity grew, and the more I learned about Saint Augustine and other philosophers and theologians, the more I realized that his influence spans beyond me as an individual. I discovered that Saint Augustine's influence played a major role in the shaping of Western philosophical history and worldview. When I later read about Saint Thomas Aquinas or Saint Bonaventure or Saint Dominic, there was once again mention of Saint Augustine and his influence on them even centuries later. It's like running into a friend who knows this other friend, and as soon as you learn of that connection, your bond with that friend gets stronger.

This story of mine is not unique because I came to find

out that there are others who have experienced the same kind of *bookstore moment*. They walk into a bookstore casually, not much of a spiritual person, and sometimes not much of a reader either, but by God's grace, they pick up some random book off the shelf and then, all of a sudden, their life is transformed and never the same as before. I've talked to many of my peers who've had that same experience, but one notable story that you can access and read about is the story of Professor Scott Sullivan. Professor Sullivan was a guest on EWTN's *Life on the Rock* show in 2015, where he talked about his own unforgettable experience as a young college student having a bookstore moment. It is remarkably similar to my moment with Saint Augustine, except the book he randomly picked up was by Peter Kreeft—another outstanding and influential Catholic author. During this particular EWTN show, he stated with enthusiasm that this one book changed his life! After that one bookstore moment, not only did he pursue the trail to convert to the Catholic faith, but he also became a daily practitioner of the faith as well as a Catholic philosopher, teaching others about God.

There's something about these spiritual books that profoundly touches our hearts and our minds. For me, reading Saint Augustine is like having a conversation with Saint Augustine himself. There he was, this spiritual giant of the Western world and of Church history, telling me his story, his personal struggles, his inner thoughts, and what he had to do in order to do God's will. Right then, I realized how blessed I was to have a such a personal encounter with him through his books. Reading a lot of his work felt like I was meeting this rock star in person, having a one-on-one conversation with him, getting to know him really well, and getting advice from him on how to navigate through life.

This specific encounter with Saint Augustine, and then eventually with Saint Thomas Aquinas, Saint Francis, and Saint Dominic, enabled me to realize that I have been overlooking the details of how these great saints came to be. Prior to reading Saint

Augustine, I knew him only by name. I knew nothing about him other than that he was a saint and a highly revered figure in the Catholic Church and that parishes and cities were named after him. It was only after reading his book that I realized that there was a lot more to him than just a name and a saintly historical figure. The more you read his accounts of his early life, the more you will realize that Saint Augustine was human after all, and with some very earthy human frailties. Augustine, a church leader, a canonized saint, and regarded by many people as holy, was also once an ordinary, sinful human being. His struggles were the same as yours and mine. He struggled with life in ways that you and I can actually relate to. But all this would have been unbeknownst to me if I had not tried to get to know him better by reading his works.

And it is not just Augustine. There is something about the wisdom of saints. What did the saints know that we need to know? They have figured out some of life's complexities and we need to tap into what they know. Remember that they also walked this earth as ordinary human beings. Reading the lives of the saints, particularly the details of their preconversion stories, we discover that despite the many grand things they have done in serving God and their fellow human beings, at many points in their lives, they were also very human. They were just as ordinary as you and me. But they did it. They did great things for God and for others, and they became saints. But we wouldn't know what they did unless we did some digging ourselves. In their stories is where we will see how they came to be saints. We will learn how it is possible for us to become saints too. Reading is like having a personal conversation with the author. It is like an opportunity for us to ask them how they did the things they did. What did they do when certain situations arose? How did they persevere? What motivated them to pursue holiness? What did they have to do to pursue holiness? What was the reason they got up every morning?

BJ Gonzalvo, Ph.D.

We should all be curious to know what got them to where they are now—heaven. For that, too, is the destination that beckons us all.

As we further explore the lives of the saints, we will find their stories and their moments of struggles to be moments that we can all relate to in our own lives. If we only took the time to get to know the saints more and explore the details of their lives, we might just find spiritual inspiration for our own daily grind. And not only will their lives bring us inspiration but they might also help us realize that the call they were responding to is also the same call we hear daily in our own lives. That call to holiness is also ours to hear. And just as the lives of the saints reveal, that call can be found not just in the big moments but in the small, ordinary moments of everyday life.

When I taught Sunday school many years ago, I would ask the class of young teenagers who their favorite saint was. Many kids would holler, often with exuberance, "Saint Francis!" That does not surprise me because Saint Francis is one of the most popular saints we have today. We know Saint Francis especially now that we have our Pope named after him. When I asked the follow-up question of what they knew about Saint Francis, the reply I got was not at all that surprising either.

Some kids would say Saint Francis took care of the animals.
Others would say that he loved the birds and even the wolves.
A few kids would say that Saint Francis cared for the poor.

We have a few tidbits of information about this popular saint, but I'm afraid that not many people know about the details of his life and how he became a saint. There are so many things we have yet to learn about Saint Francis. He has so much wisdom to share with us if only we spend more time getting to know him. We all get very busy in life. We don't often get the time or the luxury to get the chance to really delve in and get to know saints on a more personal level. Other life priorities tend to take over, and we get very busy—too busy to learn about the saints.

But I hope we take the time to get to know the saints more, for there is a whole lot more to know about them. There's a lot more to Saint Francis than just being a lover of animals. There is a lot more to Saint Patrick than just the guy we celebrate in March when we wear green and drink merrily. There is a lot more to Saint Nicholas than being the big, jolly guy in the red suit who comes around at Christmas time to hand out gifts to little children. We just have to squeeze into our busy schedules some time to get to know the saints, for there is so much wisdom and valuable life lessons that we can take away from their lives and their journeys.

Meet My Friend Jay

Several years ago, I met a young man; let's call him Jay. Jay is now one of my closest friends, but before we connected, I was reluctant to be introduced to him. Friends we had in common would tell me that I should meet him. They told me that he was "very Catholic." They said that because I guess they meant that he wasn't the type of Catholic that went to church only on Sundays. I guess they meant that he didn't just go through the motions of being a Catholic. They say he took the effort to really make time to pray. He attended daily mass and did his holy hours. And, like I was at the time, he was also considering the priestly vocation—a rare occurrence in my circle of friends, but that fact also caused me trepidation to meet him. I felt like he was too busy in prayer and too busy pursuing holiness and that I shouldn't try to take up some of his time and energy. I asked myself why someone so prayerful like him would even try to be buddies with an ordinary sinner like me. I felt like I might just get in his way. Still, the thought of talking about our experiences pushed me to call him up and meet with him in person. I thought maybe I would even draw some inspiration from him and even learn a few things.

After some days mulling it over, I eventually picked up the

phone to give him a call. We talked. I introduced myself; I told him that I too was considering the priesthood. I asked him how his vocational discernment was going. I told him how much other people had spoken so highly of him and that had made me really eager to meet him. That phone call was just a start. We eventually met in person. We ended up hanging out more, and I got to know him better. In fact, we became the best of friends. Twenty-something years have passed, and today I still consider him to be one of my closest friends and we would catch up every once in a while. Looking back to the days prior to our meeting, I didn't have grounds to feel so reluctant and intimidated to get to know him because the more I got to know him, the more I realized he was just like me. As a close friend of his over the years, I got to witness his daily struggles for holiness and came to realize that his struggles were not that different from mine. I found his journey to be totally relatable. To me, he is, after all, a very real and down-to-earth person. Through my long and close friendship with Jay, I realized that we—and really, all of us—are all on the same journey, all called to be saints. Some of us might be steps ahead in this journey, but it is not a race. Because what matters more is that we are all called to the same destination.

    I use this real-life example to illustrate that getting to know the saints takes a similar process. We have to actively pursue it. Don't hesitate to get to know the saints. Go ahead and pick up that book about the saints that you've always wondered about and allow them to introduce themselves to you. The saints are a lot more than just parish names or city names. They are a lot more than just statues or relics. They were once real people who walked this earth and struggled with the same things with which we now struggle. Life lessons abound if we just take a closer look at their lives and what they have done in response to God's call. We have to spend time with them, get to know them, befriend them, and find things that we have in common with them. We should not be intimidated. We make the effort to spend time with people we want to know better. It's the same with the saints—we have to make the effort to spend time with them in prayer and in books. Sometimes it may take years or even a lifetime, but it is by spending time with the saints and getting to know them that we realize that we can be just like them and that we too can get on that same path to holiness. Eventually, spending time with the saints becomes effortless. They become our good friends and constant companions in life, guiding us every step of the way.

Not Always Saintly

As you get to know the saints, one thing you might learn is that some of the saints that we now deeply admire and highly revere were some of the most ordinary and even some of the most sinful human beings. Saints Francis, Saint Ignatius, and Saint Charles de Foucauld, just like Saint Augustine, were playboys and womanizers before they finally surrendered to the will of God. Remember Saint Peter, for whom the Church is built upon by Jesus Christ? In the face of persecution, he denied that he even knew Christ—not once, not twice, but three times. Saint Jerome, a Doctor of the Church and one of our early Church fathers, had a violent temper. He was a cranky fellow, difficult to get along with, and made a lot of enemies. Someone called him a "porcupine saint" because he was so prickly with the people he disagreed with. Saint Angela of Foligno, a recently canonized saint from the Medieval period, had an obsession with luxurious living, material possessions, and earthly pleasures. Saint Ignatius, besides being a womanizer, was addicted to gambling. And there is Saint Paul, one of the most well-known saints of the New Testament and of early Christianity. Before his conversion on the road to Damascus, he was a fierce persecutor of Christians and one who approved the stoning death of Saint Stephen the Martyr.

Many saints' conversion stories are not just single-moment events like a "road to Damascus" conversion. Look below the surface and you will discover their conversions were long, arduous, turbulent, and lasting a lifetime. They would struggle long and keep backsliding. But nonetheless, they endured. They would get back up, battle their weaknesses, and persevere in their faith. But often, we just do not see that whole picture. We only see snippets of their lives. Often, we only see the glorious endings of their stories. We don't see them down in the pits. We don't see them in their moments when they have to decide whether to choose good or evil. We need to take the time and the opportunity to delve deeper into their lives to know them better and to be able to emulate their response to holiness.

The saints weren't always perfect. Yet, despite their sinfulness, they heard God's call, and they sought God's grace to see the light and overcome their frailties. They were not born holy, but they willed to be holy. How they willed to be holy is the story we need to hear, for that can serve as our guide for how to respond to God's call.

We too are all called to that same conversion every single moment in our lives. And a lot of times, that call to conversion comes when we are down in the pits. As Mother Angelica, founder of Eternal Word Television Network (EWTN), would say, "Holiness is not for wimps." The road to holiness is never easy. We cannot replicate the circumstances that the saints experienced because the Holy Spirit works uniquely in each one of us. We all have different callings in life. We may not all be called to rebuild the church of San Damiano like Saint Francis, but we have our own callings to strengthen our church and our communities. We may not necessarily be called to go live in the slums of Calcutta and care for the destitute just like Mother Teresa did, but we are all called to care for the people within our reach. The calling for each one of us is right here, right now. Whether we are serving the poor, caring for the sick, or even if we are on our way to an office meeting or watching our kid's soccer game, the call to saintliness is right here, right now. Right where we are is our proving ground. We do not have to hide away in the mountains in seclusion to pursue opportunities to be saintly. It is true some of our greatest spiritual leaders went off into seclusion to pray. Moses went off into the mountains. Jesus went off into the wilderness. Saint Francis went off into Mount La Verna. Saint Ignatius went off into a cave. They all spent time alone to pray and meditate and then produced great works after that. However, the greatest opportunity to act and be holy was when they were back in the world, when they were with the people, when they were doing their work in the world. The mundane tasks we face might not be the grand, monumental task that the hero in each one of us looks for, but whatever that task is, we need to recognize that the call to saintliness is right there in those daily, mundane moments.

The call for us to pursue saintliness is constant, and we just have to open our hearts, our minds, and our ears to hear it, to understand it, and to embrace it. Brother Lawrence, the seventeenth-century monk who wrote the Catholic spiritual classic, *Practice in the Presence of God*, realized in his journey to holiness that he should learn not to differentiate between praying and doing chores. Brother Lawrence, an ex-soldier who fought in the Thirty Years' War in France, as a monk was assigned dishwasher duties by his superiors. Some of us might not easily accept such lowly duties as dishwashing but it was a calling that Brother Lawrence took to heart and even cherished. It was in those mundane moments that he recognized that God is present and that He is intimately with us. Brother Lawrence found God even amongst the pots and the pans. Brother Lawrence said, "Our actions should unite us with God when we are involved in our daily activities, just as our prayers unite us with him in our quiet devotions."[1] The opportunity to be in the presence of God is everywhere, and we simply need to recognize it, just like Brother Lawrence did.

It is comforting to know that we have the saints to look up to, to ask for prayers and intercessions, and to model after because they have been there before. They want to share with us, their younger brothers and sisters in Christ on earth, how to respond to God's call for us. They responded to God's call and did so with faithfulness, with perseverance over their human weaknesses, and with joyfulness. By looking at the details of the lives of the saints, not only will we realize how much of a connection we have with them, but we will also discover that it is not that impossible to become like them. Let's take it one small step at a time. Let's try to find God in the small moments. Let's learn to listen to God's call, even if that call is as ordinary as washing dishes. Let's learn to say yes to God even in the smallest and most ordinary moments because holiness starts there. Those small moments are filled with God's love trying to reach out to us. And by starting small, we might just realize that holiness is not that impossible or far-fetched. We see in the details of the lives of the saints, even in their dishwashing moments, that it is totally doable for us to recognize God's presence and continuously strive for sanctity.

> *The saints have no need of honor from us; neither does our devotion add the slightest thing to what is theirs. Clearly, if we venerate their memory, it serves us, not them.*
>
> *—Saint Bernard of Clairvaux*

---

[1] Fourth Conversation in *The Practice of the Presence of God*, by Brother Lawrence (New Kensington, PA: Whitaker House, 1982).

Called to Be Holy, Called to Be a Leader

Inherent in the saints' response to the call to holiness is the responsibility to lead. As Saint Francis of Assisi realized the need to serve the poor, as Mother Teresa realized the need to serve the sick and the dying, and as Saint John Bosco realized the need to serve the children of the streets, their call to be leaders emerged. They became leaders and founders because it was necessary to fulfill the vision that God had entrusted to them. Their leadership potential surfaced and developed organically out of their responsiveness to what God was calling them to do.

The call to lead, just like the call to be a saint, is not an easy calling, and many of us tend to shy away from both callings. Many of us tend to deny that we are called to be a leader even though there are not that many roles in life that do not involve being a leader. Being a parent is a call to leadership. Being a big brother or sister is a call to leadership. Many of the roles we have in our lives are leadership roles even though we do not necessarily see them that way. Robert McKenna, professor of industrial/organizational psychology at Seattle Pacific University and author of the book *Dying to Lead: Sacrificial Leadership in a Self-Centered World*,[2] described leadership as responsibility—meaning that if you are responsible for others, even if you are responsible for just one person, then you are a leader. If we do not feel that we have that responsibility, we just need to pause and think about our loved ones, our neighbors, our coworkers, our friends, etc. That means all of us, with or without a formal leadership title, are called to be leaders. As Ralph Melvin Stogdil and Bernard M. Bass wrote, "Leadership is a universal human phenomenon."[3] Since ancient

---

[2] McKenna, R. *Dying to Lead: Sacrificial Leadership in a Self-Centered World* (Xulon Press: 2008).
[3] Ralph Melvin Stogdill and Bernard M. Bass, *Bass and Stogdill's Handbook of Leadership: Theory, Research, and Managerial Applications,* 3rd Ed. (NY: The Free Press, 1990), 5.

times, civilizations around the world have been grappling with leadership. Leadership is something that is deeply ingrained in our nature as human beings. God calls us to be saints, but what that call entails is the call to lead. The call to saintliness, in so many ways, is one and the same as the call to lead. The call to be saintly is inherently a call to be a leader that inspires people to want to follow. It is our responsibility as Christians to show the world the love of Christ and to inspire others. When the saints tried to respond to the call to holiness, leadership naturally followed because they wanted to share with others the love of Christ. As Saint Joan of Arc responded to the call of God to save France, leadership happened. Saint Joan of Arc became a leader, leading her army to many victories. As Saint Francis, Saint Ignatius, and Saint Dominic tried to respond to God's call to holiness, people followed them and hence started their respective religious orders. They didn't start out wanting to be leaders. Saint Francis, for instance, was clear about not being a leader. He never wanted to be the superior, even of the religious group that he himself founded, and yet people, millions of people throughout history, chose to follow his lead. Saint Francis and many of the other saints responded to God's calling, and as a result, they became not only saints but also leaders—extraordinary leaders.

We have not traditionally looked to the saints for leadership examples. When we think of leadership, what generally comes to mind are figures like CEOs, military leaders, or presidents. However, we cannot brush off the saints' leadership examples anymore. Their leadership ways are actually some of the best examples of what true leadership is. They didn't provide us explicit written works about how to lead. They didn't write how-to manuals on leadership just like how many of the leadership experts do now. Instead, their leadership lessons are etched in their lives and in their deeds.

God's call for both of these vocations, saintliness and leadership, is not reserved for the chosen few; it is not just for the saints. It is a call for all of us. And the next time you hear that call to step up to the leadership plate, whether at work, at school, at home, or anywhere that needs your leadership, do not hesitate to call on the saints. We usually call on the saints for prayer or for guidance, but we can also call on them for some real-life examples of leadership.

> *We are all called to be saints.*
> *Don't miss the opportunity.*
>
> *—Mother Angelica of EWTN*

The Leadership Search Continues

In the business world, where I have been for the last ten years, the topic of leadership is something that has always piqued the interest of many. I have attended and taught many leadership training sessions over the years and I can attest to the fact that there is a steady stream of interest in learning about leadership. In business, in politics, in religion, and in many domains of our society, there is an insatiable demand to try to tackle the topic of leadership and to figure out what leadership really is. That is understandably so because leadership is a very important position and there is a genuine need for both leaders and followers to understand it. Unfortunately, some of the insistence to understand leadership is partly due to the failings and shortcomings of many of the leaders that we have put in those positions. With so many leadership failures in recent history, we know what leadership failure looks like. It is messy and we try to do our best to understand it so that we can avoid it.

We expect a lot from our leaders. We want our leaders to be perfect and blameless. We want our leaders to have all the answers. We put a lot on our leaders' shoulders. We try to do our best in selecting the individuals for leadership positions, but time and time again, we misjudge. We get disappointed by them, by their actions, and by their personas. Our skill of spotting bad leadership before they fail us is work in progress. But we keep marching on, continuing our search for the right person to come along, someone we can trust and follow. We continue to look to fill the leadership voids, often times judiciously but sometimes haphazardly.

Leadership is a perennially important topic, especially in my field of profession, business and organizational psychology. A lot of ink has been spilled on the subject. I ran a quick Amazon.com search for books about leadership, and it generated over two hundred thousand results. Many books have been written on the topic! It is also possible that there are about that same number of ways to view leadership! Needless to say, it is clearly an important topic and will continue to be an important topic in the future.

But even with the many perspectives and taxonomies, no matter how you look at it, leadership is leadership. In the leadership literature, there tends to be a clear distinction between business leadership and the kind of leadership that exists in religious circles. In the business world, we have certain expected traits and qualities from our leaders. We often expect them to be results oriented and focused on the bottom line. In the religious arena, we also have a certain set of expectations from our leaders. We expect them to have, among others, heroic, self-sacrificing traits. There seems to be that imaginary line between religion and business, politics, and virtually every other aspect of our society. However, if we boil leadership down to its very core, what we will find is that leadership, in any of the domains, has the same fundamental characteristics and the same elemental composition—the same elements that are universally applicable no matter what the situation is. At its core, leadership is leadership, no matter how we understand it. At its very essence, leadership is defined by key characteristics such as authenticity, vision, purpose, humility, service, strength, perseverance, and selflessness. In much of the leadership studies conducted in the last century, these are the key leadership characteristics that consistently appear to be important. There is something very fundamental about these traits, and there is no doubt that we will continue to keep searching for them in our leaders.

Through these traits, we set the standards for what we expect our leaders to be. We constantly search for leaders with these characteristics, even though many of us know that with the many failings at the leadership position, these are characteristics that are just difficult to find. Perhaps some of us have come to a point of realization that great leaders just don't come around too often anymore. And for those of us aspiring to become leaders, we have become disillusioned in our search for good leadership models to follow.

However, there is no need to despair. The demand for great leaders has always been and will always be there but history has shown us, time and time again, that there are individuals who step forward and stand up to the demands of leadership. There are individuals who have demonstrated for us that there are proven and time-tested leadership models out there for us after all. We just need to know where to look for such models. And we don't need to look very far. We are blessed to have such models in our Church and all we need to do is revisit the timeless richness of the lives of the saints. There we will find some important lessons for how we, ourselves, can navigate the leadership landscape today. The leadership that many of the saints exuded tends to get overlooked, but the ways they demonstrated leadership can give us a fresh take on what it really takes to be a leader.

Take authentic leadership, for example. There's a big buzz around what authentic leadership is. In today's world, we're always looking for authentic leadership—leadership that can be trusted. If we explore and examine the kinds of leadership that the saints exuded, what we will find are the kinds of leadership that was organic and authentic. Their leadership was organic in the sense that their acts of leading emerged out of the necessities of their situation. They sensed the need to act and they took the lead to step forward. The saints were first striving not for leadership but for holiness, for they were simply responding to what God was calling them to do; but along the way in their response, they ended up responding to the call to be leaders. Their kind of leadership is what we call "emergent leadership." They weren't necessarily striving for leadership positions, but their leadership emerged out of the situations that they were in—the situations where they were full-heartedly and authentically responding to the call of God.

Emergent leadership, according to a 2014 *Washington Post* article, is actually one of the key characteristics that some of the most innovative companies look for in today's complex environments.[4] Leaders can and should come from any level, even the lowest level of the organization. When the situation arises, individuals must emerge and be willing to take up the responsibility and lead as the situation calls for, no matter where they are in life. Whether they are a boss, a clerk, or a servant, when the opportunity comes, they should be ready to emerge as a leader.

Called by Jesus to take care of His sheep and to follow Him (John 21:16–19), Simon Peter stepped up to emerge as the leader of the disciples after Jesus died. He had some weaknesses and imperfections, but when Jesus entrusted him with the leadership position, he responded with maturity and faithfulness, assured that he was doing what Christ had asked him to do.

Along with emergent leadership, the saints exuded some of the best examples of leadership for many different and often difficult situations. They did not simply intend to have people follow

---

[4] Matt McFarland, "Emergent leadership: The trait that smart, innovative companies seek out in employees." *The Washington Post,* February 24, 2014.

them, but because of their authentic and the organic leadership characteristics that emerged out of the situational needs, people were drawn to follow them. People were drawn to follow their lead. People mustered up to help them respond to the situations at hand.

In the slums of Calcutta, a hundred people needed to be fed, but people recognized that one person cannot do it alone. Others realized it and also saw that need, and so they stepped up to follow the lead of one authentic nun, Mother Teresa, who was trying to solve that problem.

Mother Teresa is usually not the first to come to mind when it comes to imagining a leader today. She is the first to come to my mind when it comes to prayer, service, or holiness, but not when it comes to being a leader of a large multinational organization. Mother Teresa is, in fact, a great exemplary leader. She led one of the largest global organizations ever to have existed. It's the same with Saint Francis, Saint Dominic, and Saint Ignatius—all founders of large global organizations that still continue to thrive today.

The saints, as we already know, were inspirational. Who wouldn't be moved by Saint Paul's tireless dedication to spreading the gospel? Who wouldn't be moved by Mother Teresa's compassion for every homeless person she encountered in the streets of Calcutta? Who wouldn't be moved by the humbleness of Saint Francis? Or by the grit of Saint Ignatius? Or by the courageousness of Saint Joan of Arc? Or by the insightful spirituality of Saint Therese of Lisieux? Their own personal ways of responding to the call to holiness are undeniably just truly amazing. But as we look to the saints for inspiration on how to live a truly Christian life, what we will also find are some true and authentic leadership examples that we can use today.

For many of us looking for leadership examples, we don't need to look any further. The saints have, all this time, been there waiting to demonstrate, through their lives and their stories, what true leadership is. We just have to grab the chance to get to know them. Leaders like them just don't come around too often! And today we have a desperate need for the kinds of leadership qualities that they exuded. So let me invite you to join me on this journey as I revisit the lives of the saints to get a glimpse of how leadership should be.

Tolle Lege, Tolle Lege

If you have not had the chance to read about the lives of the saints, I fervently urge you to pick up one of their first-hand writings, such as Saint Augustine's *Confessions* or Saint Teresa of Avila's *The Interior Castle,* or perhaps a second-hand account writing about their lives, such as Saint Bonaventure's *The Life of Saint Francis of Assisi* or G. K. Chesterton's *Saint Thomas Aquinas,* and just start reading.

Just like that heavenly voice that Saint Augustine heard telling him "tolle lege, tolle lege." which means "take up and read." Saint Augustine listened to the voice, picked up the book the Epistle to the Romans and read it. That marked the beginning of his new life. So take up and read either an old-fashioned traditional book or a digital version or maybe listen to an audiobook. Say a little prayer to ask God for guidance and to open your heart and your mind, read the first few pages and prepare to get to know the saint deeply. Maybe it's your first reading or your second or third reading of any book about a saint, read in a different light with a fresh take. Keep on getting to know the saint more deeply. Befriend the saint just like how Father Benedict Groeschel described how he approached his relationship with the saints. The saints were his life-long friends and he had them accompany him every step of the way. Father Benedict wrote:

> "No matter who you are or what your experience is, there is a saint—and probably many saints—who will speak to you. Find those saints through study and prayer, and form relationships with them. Turn to the 'cloud of witnesses' that God has so lovingly provided for us. I guarantee your life will never be quite the same."[5]

You might be wondering if the saints are still relevant today because maybe you are thinking that they lived so long ago and that the times we are in now are very different from theirs. You might wonder how their stories would resonate with your struggles and if you actually have anything in common with the saints. Those thoughts entered my mind too, but what I found is that there is something transcendent about their stories that still deeply resonates with many of our own struggles in this day and age. Especially with the various distractions that we now have in our society, constantly pulling us away from knowing the love of God, the timeless wisdom of the saints is actually just what we need in our world today.

Light of the World, Salt of the Earth

> *What I have written will do a lot of good. It will make the kindness of God better known.*
>
> —Saint Therese of Lisieux

---

[5] Groeschel, Benedict. *The Saints in My Life: My Favorite Spiritual Companions* (Huntington, IN: Our Sunday Visitor, 2011), 201.

We have a very rich source of wisdom in the saints. There are over ten thousand canonized saints, and I don't think I'll ever get to know about each and every one of them in my lifetime. Nonetheless, even with the few saints that we will get to know, there is a wealth of examples of leadership for us to discover in their lives. And what a rewarding experience it is to go digging into their lives for those nuggets of wisdom! I hope that in this book I am able to illustrate how the saints practiced and demonstrated both holiness and leadership in their lives for we can truly use their examples in our own lives. Using this fresh lens of looking at the lives of the saints, we can use their examples for how we ourselves can draw out our own leadership potential at work, at home, in our communities, in our circles of influence, and virtually in every aspect of our everyday lives.

Lumen Gentium, one of the principal documents of the Second Vatican Council in the 1960s, calls us, the laity, to bring faith to the world; and that it is our role to make Christ known to others by the way we live our own everyday lives. I grew up as part of the JP2 Generation (John Paul II Generation), and I am inspired and empowered by Pope John Paul II's message, especially the main message at World Youth Day 2002 in Toronto, for us to be the "salt of the earth, the light of the world." And I invoke the help of the saints to garner even more light so that together we can make that light stronger and brighter. I would like to use their stories to shine a light on our paths to leadership and to oneness with God. I wish to invoke the help of the saints to also be the salt of this earth. We use salt now to add flavor to our food, but salt, particularly in the ancient days, was also used to preserve the meat and the fish from spoiling. We turn to the saints to help us preserve the teachings of Christ and to keep our society from spoiling and going bad.

One of the most effective ways to learn leadership and be an effective leader is by modeling after the successful examples of others. Leadership does not have to be learned by reading some textbook, attending a training course, or coaching and mentoring.

These methods are fine, but one of the most potent ways to learn leadership is by modeling the examples of others. It is a more effective training tool than sending students to a classroom to sit and listen to a lecture on leadership.

In the social learning theory by Albert Bandura, one of the most influential psychologists of our time, human beings are active information processors. According to the social learning theory, we process information by observing, connecting the event with the context of the event, remembering, and then using that information to reproduce that same behavior observed.[6] We can model our behaviors from leadership figures who get our attention, especially when we make the connections between their behaviors and the rewards they received. We are motivated by those connections to act and behave in similar ways, knowing that the reward of oneness with God is all we need.

The saints serve as radiant models of the faith, but more specifically, as this book wishes to illustrate, they modeled for us how it is to follow Christ and how it is to lead our brothers and sisters in Christ. This book is meant to offer examples and inspirations from the saints so that the readers will be motivated to unleash their own leadership potential to respond to the challenges and to lead and influence others. When it comes to leadership, along with their faith and virtues, the saints certainly talked the talk and walked the walk. They were men and women of actions in the real world who faced some of the most difficult challenges. They led armies. They fought social injustice. They served the poor. They cared for the sick and the dying where no one else would. They carried out their faith in God and their love for God all the way through. They demonstrated authentic leadership by example, and they lived out their leadership principles all the way to the end of their earthly lives.

---

[6] Bandura, Albert. *Social Learning Theory* (New York: General Learning Press, 1972).

In virtually every aspect of societal life, there will always be a need for leadership. In battles, in business operations, in church ministry, people will always look for leadership. There will always be an interest in finding good, reliable, and trustworthy leadership. We will continue to want to know what to look for in our leaders and in our choosing of our leaders. Scholars will continue to spill ink on this topic of leadership. This book, however, is not meant to spill more ink trying to add another theory about leadership or to add another definition of leadership. What this book invites you to do is to consider leadership from a different and fresh perspective. With the leadership crisis that we have experienced over the centuries, it is time that we take a look at leadership through a different kind of lens. It is not necessarily a novel perspective because it is a perspective that really goes back to the times of Jesus and the centuries where we got to witness great, inspirational leadership. If anything, it's a fresh take.

A lot of the leadership research done in recent decades has been from the perspective of business and management. This book will look at leadership from that angle too because it is important that we become more aware of how leadership is traditionally viewed, how we have arrived as a society to come to that view, and how people are stepping up to leadership positions with that fundamental view. But in addition to the traditional ways we view leadership, we will look at leadership from another perspective, one that is a bit atypical but nonetheless important: through the leadership lens enlightened and colored with examples from the lives of the saints.

WWJD? Ask the Saints

Remember the popular bracelets that came out in the 1990s that said "WWJD?" Well, even though the bracelet has run out of style, that question "What Would Jesus Do?" remains timeless. It is a question that we should constantly be asking ourselves. And just who can we ask? We can ask the saints. They pondered that same question and found some answers. And they can show us some of the answers they discovered.

If we hold true to the saying "Lead by example," then the saints are some of the greatest and truest exemplary leaders. Their following of the footsteps of Christ and the lives they lived, through the best of times and the worst of times, demonstrated leadership that is bound to inspire and motivate the faithful who are also striving to follow the footsteps of Christ.

Thank you to our older brothers and sisters in Christ who have gone before us and have shown us the way. The saints, though they might not fit the traditional leadership box, were true leaders, leading from the front, and they leave us with great examples that we can follow and emulate today. They courageously stepped up to respond to the call of Christ to follow Him; and as they did so, they inspired and garnered others to follow their lead toward sanctity. As the saints stepped forward to respond to the call of Christ and to follow Christ, our one great leader, they, in turn, became leaders themselves.

I pray and hope that this book can serve as an invaluable resource for someone looking for leadership examples and inspiration for how to lead—how to lead others and how to lead oneself to living a meaningful life. This book is intended not just for Catholic readers but for anyone with an interest in leadership and looking for inspiring and effective models to emulate. As aspiring leaders, we often like to look for leadership examples and templates that we can use and model after. We like to look for examples that are proven to work. Well, pause your search here and consider the saints. The lives of the saints are full of leadership examples. Their lives are like a gold mine full of examples for what to do in so many situations, including situations in our modern lives. And I wish that this book will simply be an echo of the ways the saints lived their lives and the ways they led others. This book is intended to help the readers discover how the saints' examples can serve as our model and markers for our own roadmap as we navigate our own leadership paths. I hope that reading about the saints will be a great source of inspiration, courage, and wisdom for us inspiring leaders.

I hope that your reading will yield the same results just as when the saints read books about other saints. After all, many of the saints became saints themselves after reading about the lives of the saints who lived before them. They drew inspiration from their predecessors' exemplary lives. The founder of the Jesuits, Saint Ignatius of Loyola, for example, found his inspiration after reading a book about the lives of Saint Francis and Saint Dominic. And we can trace back many illustrious moments in Catholic spirituality to this one simple reading. It was this one reading that inspired the many great deeds of Saint Ignatius, which in turn inspired many of us who followed him. The Jesuit universities, the *Spiritual Exercises*, and even our current Pope can all be traced back to this one simple reading. Many of the great moments in history started with a book.

It Starts with a Book

The year was 1521, about three hundred years since the passing of Saint Francis and Saint Dominic. Ignatius was serving as a military leader, fighting and defending his fortress against the French army, when all of a sudden, while in battle, a cannonball hit his leg, rendering him incapacitated. He almost lost his life. He almost lost both of his legs. He spent weeks confined in recovery, but it was actually during this time that he would discover his life's calling. While recovering from this injury and unable to walk, he decided to resort to reading books to keep him preoccupied and distracted from his disability. Being the consummate soldier and knight that he was, he looked for books on chivalry and military valor. However, the only books available to him at that time were books on the life of Christ, *Divina Christi*, and on the lives of the saints, particularly of Saints Francis and Dominic. It must have been divine intervention at work because it was not so much due to piety that he chose to read those books but simply because he had nothing else to do and nothing else to read while recovering from his battle wounds. Divine providence, again in its own mysterious ways, has it that those books would have a profound impact on him and the great things that he would do in his life. Ignatius was so inspired by what he read about what Saint Francis and Saint Dominic had done in their lives to answer the call of God that he decided to imitate them. He found the inspiration for what he might want to do with his young life. He said to himself, "Saint Dominic did this; therefore I must do it. Saint Francis did this; therefore I must do it." He did have worldly ambitions and aspirations for military valor prior to reading about Saint Francis and Saint Dominic, but instead, because of the new circumstances he was in, he completely changed course, cast aside his worldly desires and even his impieties, and gave his all to doing the work of God. With his newfound fervor on this readjusted vocation, he would go living the rest of his life striving for holiness with a burning desire to serve as a soldier for Christ.

It was a profound spiritual journey for him, and we have him to thank for writing down his spiritual experiences and share with us his thoughts on the path to a deeper relationship with God. His writings would eventually lead to one of the most fruitful and famous works in Christianity, a book that has been widely used by many Christians throughout the centuries as a spiritual guide, *The Spiritual Exercises of Saint Ignatius*.

He also founded one of the most successful and largest Catholic organizations in the world today, the Society of Jesus, also known as the Jesuits. His life was consecrated to doing the work of the society he founded, embracing the vows of chastity, poverty, and obedience in imitation of the life of Jesus Christ. Today, the society remains strong and one of the largest Catholic organizations, with over sixteen thousand members worldwide. They continue to do God's work, adhering to the visions that Saint Ignatius laid out almost five hundred years ago. His book, the *Spiritual Exercises*, continues to provide guidance and serve as a how-to manual for Christians wishing to deepen their relationship with God. He also had a profound impact on his followers and contemporaries, particularly on another saint, Francis Xavier, who himself also became an influential missionary who had a profound impact on the spread of Catholicism in Asia. But if you trace back all these wonderful and amazing works for God by Saint Francis Xavier, by Saint Ignatius, and by other Jesuits throughout history, all of it can be traced back to a book.

Sometimes, our leadership potential emerges by the simple act of reading an inspirational book. Some say that deep reading is going into extinction and that people nowadays are reading less. We have so many other things in our society trying to grab our attention and deep reading becomes less of a priority but when you get the chance to sit down and immerse yourself in a book, pick something about the saints. We have heard the cliché that books change lives. In this case, books about the saints have the power to change lives and have definitely done so. They inspire and ignite others to act, to serve, and to follow the path to holiness.

Saint Josemaria Escriva said, "Reading has made many saints." We see that in Saint Ignatius's story of reading about Saints Francis and Dominic. And as mentioned previously in this book, Saint Augustine's conversion journey began after hearing the voice to take up and read the Epistle to the Romans.

Saint Edith Stein, or also known as Saint Teresa Benedicta of the Cross, before she converted to Catholicism in the early 1900s, happened to pick up the autobiography of sixteenth-century Carmelite nun Saint Teresa of Avila at a friend's house. She began to read right then and there. That one fateful night, she read the entire book, and when she finished, she closed it and said, "This is the truth." Her life's direction then became clear. She had a very strong Jewish background growing up, but at the age of thirty-one, she converted and was baptized Roman Catholic. Several years later, she entered the Carmelite monastery to become a nun, taking the religious name Teresa Benedicta of the Cross. Her fascinating spiritual journey started with a book.

The saints' life stories are stories that we need to keep retelling time and time again. It is my hope for this book to be able to tell their stories and to shine at least even a fraction of the brilliance of their lives. I wish to have the readers be inspired as I simply echo the stories of the saints, sometimes in a different light—a different light that highlights their leadership. And I hope that upon reading this book, readers will become inspired to be leaders, not only in the modern sense of what leadership is, but to be leaders in the way the saints exuded leadership. I hope that as you read the pages of this book, you will find a connection to their lives and that their stories resonate with you, with your everyday experiences. I invite you to have a conversation with the saints. Let's listen to their stories and find inspiration for our daily lives today.

Storytelling is powerful. We human beings respond to stories in a way that we read and immerse ourselves as if we are personally part of that story. We tend to ground those stories that we hear about within our own personal experiences. So, through this book and my exploration of the lives of the saints, I hope that you can join me in immersing ourselves in the ocean of wisdom of the saints and learn some valuable lessons in leadership that we can apply in our lives today. Especially in this day and age, we need to hear the saints' life stories. Anthropologists and social scientists believe that storytelling is and has always been an important human activity because it allows us to learn from the lessons that our fellow human beings have already learned, even from long ago. Some of life's best lessons can be learned from the saints because they have been there and done it, and they can show us the way.

Many of us have heard the stories of the saints, but very few have told those stories about their leadership. So, as I retell the stories of the saints in this book about leadership, allow me to echo what Saint Francis of Assisi used to say to his friars: "Come along; I'll show you how." Allow me to show you how they led and how we can use their leadership examples in our own lives. Let's look for those nuggets of leadership wisdom and find out what makes the leadership style of the saints an effective model for us to follow.

You don't have to be a leader holding an official leadership position. Anyone should be able to lead. One should not need a title to lead. We should all have a vision to lead, to inspire, and to make a difference. We should all be empowered and inspired to lead. And people who already are leaders with a title or an office, heed the saying of what Saint Augustine would say to his fellow bishops: "No man can be a good bishop if he loves his title but not his task." Just like what leadership gurus John Maxwell and Robin Sharma have said, leadership is not about the title. Leadership is about what you do as a leader, how you are making an impact on the world, how you influence other people's lives, and how you inspire others to act.

Many say that leadership is influence. And if leadership is influence, then there is definitely something about the saints who have profoundly influenced others and continue to have a lasting influence on so many people even years after their death. They have incited and continue to incite their followers to be leaders themselves. One of the leading authorities on leadership, Tom

Peters, said, "Leaders don't create followers; they create more leaders."

In the case of Saint Francis, for example, many of his followers have emerged as leaders. The leadership that Saint Francis exuded eight hundred years ago was a gift that keeps on giving even unto this day. He inspired Saint Ignatius, who inspired Saint Francis Xavier, who inspired Mother Teresa, who inspired Pope Francis. Leader after leader created followers, but more important, their leadership created more leaders, who in turn created more leaders.

Leadership is contagious. According to research by Zenger and Folkman, there is scientific evidence of a correlation between leaders and their subordinates' behaviors and performance,[7] proving the point that what we do as leaders truly make a difference. How we behave, whether good or bad, gets passed on to others, implicitly or explicitly. And then it gets passed on to others, then to still more. Leadership behavior is as contagious as a smile. Smile at others, and they will likely smile at others that they meet. Lead positively, and your followers will likely lead positively.

The saints have a lot to teach us about how to lead, inspire, and influence others. We just have to allow those leadership lessons to reach our hearts and minds. And when they do reach us, we too can become saintly leaders. We too can respond to the same calling to lead and to the same calling to be holy. The call to lead and the call to be holy are always beckoning. The opportunities, as well as the potential to lead are always open to us. Remember that leadership is a calling for all of us.

You can lead, inspire, and influence wherever you are and whoever you are. You can lead by nurturing your social relationship with other people at work, at home, at church, or in your own communities. Whether it be in the workplace, in our home, or in

---

[7] Zenger, J. & Folkman, J. "The Trickle Down Effect of Good (and Bad) Leadership." Harvard Business Review (January 14, 2016).

our communities, there is a need for leadership. On every level of an organization, there is a leadership role waiting for us.

*Come, Holy Spirit, fill the hearts of the faithful
and enkindle in them the fire of Thy love.
Send forth Thy Spirit and they shall be created.
And Thou shalt renew the face of the earth.
O God, who didst instruct the hearts of the faithful
by the light of the Holy Spirit, grant us in the
same Spirit to be truly wise, and ever to rejoice
in His consolation, through Christ our Lord.
Amen*

SAINTLINESS AND LEADERSHIP

Most High, glorious God, enlighten the darkness of our minds. Give us a right faith, a firm hope and a perfect charity, so that we may always and in all things, act according to Your holy will. Amen.

—*Saint Francis of Assisi*

For centuries, we have looked to the saints for prayers, intercessions, healing, and guidance on just about everything in life, from how to worship God to how we must go about our relationships with one another, and even to finding missing keys. One of my first encounters with a saint was when I was a young teenager getting ready for Confirmation. Part of traditional Confirmation practice is to choose a saint who you would like to be named after. One usually chooses a saint who might have provided some inspiration or a saint who has had some influence on the individual. Well, I took the easy route of simply looking at whose feast day my birthday fell on. All I had to do was look in a book about Catholic saints, and there it was—November 30 is the feast day of Saint Andrew. I read a brief biography on Saint Andrew the Apostle, and I thought to myself, *Saint Andrew was not a bad choice, so why not?* I chose the name Andrew to be my confirmation name. It was a quick and easy decision for me, but in retrospect, I made it too easy for myself. I took an uninspired short cut, and it just didn't challenge me enough to get to know anything else about Saint Andrew or any of the other saints I could have chosen. Little did that teenage me know that I would one day be tremendously curious about Saint Andrew and all the other saints. Fast forward a few decades, and here I am writing about them, wonderfully awed by them, their lives, and the wisdom that they try to impart upon us.

Over all those years, I did learn one more thing about the saints. Besides being our Confirmation buddies and prayer buddies, and besides being radiant models of faith, spirituality, and virtue, there is one more critical facet of life that the saints can help us with, and that is leadership. Leadership is something we don't typically associate with the saints, but leadership should correspond to saintliness. Leadership and saintliness must go hand-in-hand because the call to saintliness is, in many ways, a call to lead.

And just like the opportunities to become saints, the opportunities to become leaders are also abundant. The call to be holy and the call to lead are all around us. However, when we choose to respond, we don't always know how. We struggle to find the right model of leadership for the opportunity. As a society, we've always been in constant search of leadership and leadership models to follow, but unfortunately, great leadership models are hard to find. The saints are not always the first to come to mind when it comes to picturing a leader, but today's society can greatly benefit from the leadership examples of the saints. Many of the saints founded and led successful and enduring organizations, and many of them still continue to have a lasting influence on people's lives today, even beyond their living years. Many of them didn't purposely set out to be leaders, but if we examine what true leadership is, we will see that these saints were true leaders and that they exhibited some of the most admirable characteristics that we look for in our leaders today. The saints leave us with some of the best timeless templates for how to lead. Their leadership, the heroic, humble, and saintly type of leadership may not be the leadership style we imagine in today's highly competitive, very business-driven, profit-driven atmosphere, but there is something profound and extraordinary about the leadership models of the saints. Something very fundamental. Something very human. Something very holy and set apart. Something very *good*.

Saints are people set apart because they are holy. The word *holy* means "set apart." And just like holiness, leaders are also set apart from the rest. We often choose our leaders because they stand out above the rest. If we just keep probing and examining the lives of the saints, we will realize that saintliness and leadership are actually compatible, complementary, and even fundamentally one and the same. The call to saintliness comes with the call to lead. The saints were first responding to their own call to holiness before they became leaders. They became leaders on their way to holiness.

If you're like me, you might be inclined to think that it is hard enough to become a leader let alone become a saint but why bother to pursue both? Saintliness and leadership are probably two of the most difficult, most demanding, and most ambitious roles we could ever go for. Why take the time and effort to be like the saints or be a leader? And why even bother to look to the saints for models when we know that it is even more difficult and even more ambitious to be a saint?

Some people will probably get intimidated by these high ideals of being a saint, but as we explore the lives of the saints, what we will find is that saintliness is not as impossible as we think. The saints too were ordinary and imperfect human beings, just like us. Leadership too, just like saintliness, is also not necessarily reserved for the elite and the extraordinary. Leaders are also ordinary and imperfect human beings. But just like how we are all called to be saints, we are also called to be leaders. Yes, you and I are called to be both saints and leaders. It is not an easy calling but, yes, ordinary folks like us are called to live up to our full potential and be extraordinary. When we build up our saintly lives, we also build up our leadership abilities. When we are responding to the call of God to greatness, we are also responding to the call to invite others to be great. And that is what leaders do—leaders invite others to be great.

So why not look to the saints for how to become saintly and how to become leaders? Let us examine how the saints responded to the call to holiness and to leadership. Let us further explore some of those leadership examples, some of the leadership traits and characteristics that made the likes of Saints Joan of Arc, Francis, Dominic, John Bosco, Therese, and Mother Teresa so effective, so well-loved, and so admired by millions of followers. Their lives are full of examples of leadership that led them ultimately to holiness. And vice versa—their lives are full of examples of holiness that led them to be leaders. Their response to the call to holiness became one and the same with their response to the call to lead. The call to lead became inherent in the call to holiness. In this present day and age where we are constantly looking up to leaders and always looking for great leaders to step up, to guide us, and to inspire us, we need to revisit the saints' lives, actions, and behaviors and see how we, living in the twenty-first century, can learn some valuable lessons in leadership that we can put into practice.

Exploring the Lives of the Saints

The saints' responses to the call to lead are some of the best examples of leadership, but it is very unlikely that you'll find case studies about their leadership in a textbook. Next time you visit a library or a bookstore, check out the business section and look for the subsection for leadership. I highly doubt that you will find anything on the leadership of a saint.

Just try to recall some of the textbooks you had in your college courses. Even if you took a business course or a leadership course, do you remember ever reading a case study on leadership where the leadership figure was a saint?

It is a rarity to find the saints' leadership examples in leadership textbooks. It's even unlikely that you'll hear the saints' examples in the conversation when talking about leadership in the classrooms or in leadership training seminars. The saints, for some reason, just do not seem to fit the traditional leadership box and are rarely considered by leadership scholars. However, what we find when we further explore the lives of the saints is that what they have demonstrated are some of the greatest leadership examples. And we are missing out if we don't take a look at the leadership lessons that they have to offer.

We live in a time when leadership has taken on far greater importance—just look at the salary big companies shell out to pay their executive leaders. The average CEO pay at the largest firms is about $16 million—that's an exponential growth by 1000 percent since the 1970s. Look also at all the leadership development programs and off-site training offered at many of our places of employment. We want everybody to maximize their leadership potential. We want every leader to be a good leader. We certainly place a high value on good leadership. But despite the leadership development programs and training, there seems to be that inevitable struggle to find good leadership. Finding or making good leaders is not always a guarantee in our society and communities. Having good leaders is undoubtedly more important than ever, and we just cannot afford to sit and wait for the next great leader to step up because the need is now, the need is greater than ever, and the need is constant. We don't just need great leaders; We need saintly leaders.

We know that even in our profit-driven culture, leadership is a lot more than just meeting the bottom line. Leadership is a lot more than just being able to produce results. Leadership is a lot more than what we currently perceive it to be. What we need is to expand our perspective and freshen up our lens so that we can look outside of the traditional leadership box and consider the examples of the saints. The saints have a lot to teach us about leadership. The saints can teach us how to respond to the call to leadership because the call to leadership is, first, a call to holiness. And in our current sources of leadership models, we just do not have a blueprint or a template for how to respond to both calls. We turn to the saints for guidance on how to respond to those calls. Let us pray to them and pray with them. Let us ask for wisdom. Let us ask the saints to help us ask God to grant us the grace so that we may open our eyes to see what it means to be a leader and a saint.

Blessed to Be Called

As Christians, we all are called to be like Christ. Christ was a leader, and therefore, we, who are called to imitate Christ are also called to imitate His leadership virtues and be leaders of our brothers and sisters. The disciples of Christ, when their leader had gone up to heaven, stepped up to leadership positions and led the other followers of Christ to know *the way, the truth, and the life*. It is our calling as followers of Christ to step up and lead wherever we may be in our lives so that others might know *the way, the truth, and the life*.

We might not be a CEO, a president, or any kind of a high-profile leader, but we might be a parent, a teacher, a student, a friend, or whatever regular, everyday role we have in life. We might not be a global leader in charge of leading thousands of people, but we are, nonetheless, in our own personal ways, all called to lead. Only a small percentage of the world population will ever become a leader on a global scale or hold a high-profile leadership role, but the call to leadership does not have to be that grandiose. Most of us live in the local and not the global.

We have the calling to lead not necessarily the entire world, but someone's world—our families, our children, our neighborhoods, our communities, etc.

All of us will have the opportunity to be a leader at some point in our lives or in someone's life. Someone, someday, will reach for our hand for guidance and for our leadership, whether as a high-profile or a low-profile leader. Consider that a blessing, a calling, and an opportunity to serve and imitate Christ. And during those times when we're searching for a leadership template to follow, we have the saints to turn to because they too, in imitation of Christ, responded to the same calling to lead. Many of the saints were not high-profile leaders but they stepped up and led successfully and effectively. They were just like many of us—ordinary. So just like those times when we turned to the saints in need of their guidance and intercessory prayers, we can, once again, turn to them to ask them to show us how to lead.

> *The good God does not need years to accomplish His work of love in a soul; one ray from His heart can, in an instant, make His flower bloom for eternity.*
>
> *—Saint Therese of Lisieux*

Formed Out of the Same Clay

Sanctity along with leadership are roles that God has called us all to. They are roles that we should and can strive for. As we explore the details of the saints' lives, we will see that their examples, especially the examples from their everyday lives, that sanctity, as well as leadership, is within our reach and that the saints themselves had to face many obstacles that we, in our modern everyday living, can relate to. Often, when we pray to the saints, we ask for their intercessions and for their guidance because they have been in our place before, and they know what it is like to face the daily challenges that we encounter in life. We understand that they too were once lost, searching for answers, and they found answers. They figured it out and came out on the other side a saint. But sometimes we forget that they were once just like us—humans. As the author of the book *Psychology of Saints*, Henri Joly, put it, "They were formed out of the same clay." The saints were once ordinary folks who walked this earth, who faced the same human dilemma, and who struggled to be holy. They were not always saintly. Being holy is not a fixed trait that people are born with.

As a young child, I used to categorize the saints along with some of the superhuman and mythological figures. I used to think that their stories belonged to the same genre as the fairy tales that I read growing up. And to some extent, many of us grown-ups have not bothered to correct such misconceptions and categorizations. Many of us still continue to think that the saints are superhuman and otherworldly.

We have to see the saints in a different light. We have to take the time and effort to get to know the saints more because becoming like them is not an impossible fairy tale. To emulate the saints is not an otherworldly ambition. The statues in the gardens, the paintings on the church walls, the stained-glass church windows, and other still images have captured them at their very best moments, the apex of their saintly lives, and we think that modeling after them just seems to be a far-fetched, fictional, improbable, impossible, and impractical idea. We have turned them into icons of perfection, but what that does is it limits our imaginations and hinders us from seeing beyond the finished product of sanctity. We need to take a closer look into the details of their lives so that we can see the journeys that they took and how they came to be. We need to see how they overcame and how they struggled for holiness in their most ordinary, mundane moments. We need to see the little moments of their decision points so that we can realize that we too are given the same opportunities to say yes to saintliness in many different moments of our own ordinary lives. If we just look deeply into the lives of the saints, we will come to realize that they were indeed very human, very ordinary, and were just as imperfect and even as sinful as us. We might then come to realize that the path they took to sanctity is also very much within our reach.

> *God would never inspire me with desires which cannot be realized; so in spite of my littleness, I can hope to be a saint.*
>
> —Saint Therese of Lisieux

The path to paradise is not easy, but if we look at the little moments, the bite-sized moments of the lives of the saints, we might be able to accept that we too can take that same approach to saintliness leading us to that same path to heavenly paradise. Many of the saints started out by doing very simple and ordinary deeds. We don't necessarily need to feed a hundred hungry people all at once, but we can start with a smaller number—even just one. As Mother Teresa said, "If you can't feed a hundred people, then just feed one." Mother Teresa got her start with just one person in need. Many of the saints got their start to the path to paradise by doing little ordinary things—doing one good deed at a time.

> *Start by doing what's necessary; then do what's possible; and suddenly you are doing the impossible.*
>
> —Saint Francis of Assisi

Saint John Bosco, who founded the religious order Salesians in 1859, started by taking care of one orphaned poor boy in need. Then three days later, he was helping nine other boys. Three months later, there were twenty-five. Now, one-hundred-plus years after his death, the religious order he founded, the Salesians, is the third largest missionary organization in the world, with almost three thousand houses that continue to serve the young people, especially the poor and the at-risk kids. Saint John Bosco lived out the words that Saint Francis of Assisi preached. Saint John Bosco started doing what was necessary, then doing what was possible, then, suddenly he was doing the impossible.

Leadership and saintliness are great tasks and might seem impossible, but they start somewhere—somewhere small and ordinary. Let us learn from Saint Therese of Lisieux, who we know for her spirituality of the "little way." It was in her little way that she manifested her love for God and for others. Whether she was doing her daily chores in the convent of Lisieux or praying with her sisters, she saw and took the opportunity to respond to the call to holiness by doing ordinary things with extraordinary love. It is in this little way where many of us can start our journeys. Saint Therese shows us that even the littlest and most ordinary things we do in our daily lives can lead us to the path to holiness.

Even in today's business world, when tackling a large complex issue, in order to reach the goal, the common wisdom is that we must approach it one step at a time, taking a more bite-sized approach. By setting smaller, incremental, and achievable goals, the larger goal becomes less daunting. When we have a lofty goal that we need to accomplish, it is almost always our natural tendency to first get overwhelmed, but sometimes that instinctive reaction leaves us so paralyzed by fear that we tend to just throw our hands up and resist engaging in the task. So we need to overcome that feeling and tackle the issue differently by looking at the small steps we can take—the winnable steps. Martin Luther King, Jr. once said that "you don't have to see the whole staircase, just take the first step." We can start goal-setting at a smaller scale and then work our way up. Let us focus on the smallest details first, perform the small tasks with love, and then work our way up to ultimately tackling the larger issue.

Everything is Impossible Until Someone Does It

The goal of becoming a saint and/or becoming a leader might seem too grand, but it is not impossible if we just try to take the first small steps—especially the first initial step. The call to be a saint and/or the call to lead is not necessarily a call to be great. The call to saintliness or leadership is a call to do small things with great efforts. They are both calls to do small things with great love. Greatness starts with the small, ordinary things. Our journeys start with the first small step, and we take one small step at a time. We can start with our own little ways. We tend to celebrate and encourage the moonshots in history, but let us not forget that a huge percentage of all the progress that has happened in the world has been the incremental progress. It is the small steps that mankind has made that have shaped much of the world we live in. Our next step to leadership or to holiness does not have to be a moonshot. It can be one small, incremental step at a time. We can lead one person at a time. We can do one holy deed at a time. The steps, even the small ones, are not easy, and that is why we have to take them one at a time. The path to saintliness and leadership is a road less traveled because it is no walk in the park; but it is, nonetheless, a road that we are all called to take. And what the saints have done by responding to God's call, often with persistence and passion, shows us that saintliness is not impossible.

Consider the story of Roger Bannister, the first sub-four-mile runner. That's right, running under four miles in one minute was once deemed impossible. Prior to 1954, the fastest mile ever in the record books was four minutes and one second. That record stood for years, and many, including doctors and scientists who conducted research and experiments, had already accepted and confirmed the fact that it was just impossible for the human body to go any faster. But then came Roger Bannister. After an unsuccessful Olympics run in 1952, he set a new goal for himself: to be the first man to run a mile in under four minutes. So, for the next two years, he trained and prepared with that goal in mind. In 1954, he did it and broke the record, becoming the first person ever to run one mile in under four minutes.

There was news coverage of it for the entire world to see. And as soon as that happened, as soon as the world witnessed that very moment, it was as if the barrier had been lifted because other runners immediately followed suit to break the sub-four-mile barrier. Year after year, runners continue to hit that mark. Today, there are thousands of individuals who have run the sub-four mile; some are even high schoolers. Roger Bannister broke not just the world record but that mental barrier that hindered runners from running such speed. He demonstrated that the impossible is possible. He opened up every runner's thinking that it could be done. It was as if everyone realized that, with training and mentality, it is certainly possible. Now average casual runners are empowered to also shoot for that goal because they know that it is not impossible as long as they set their minds to it. The moral of the story is: Everything is impossible until someone does it.

Consider again the example of Saint Ignatius. After reading about Saint Francis and Saint Dominic, Saint Ignatius thought to himself that if others can do it, why not him too? Once he found out the details of how Saint Francis and Saint Dominic became saints, he came to the realization that responding to the call to saintliness was not impossible. He realized that saintliness could be done and that he, himself, can do it. The stories of Saint Francis and Saint Dominic inspired and empowered Saint Ignatius to see that he too could do great things for God. And so off he went to jump over the barriers that hinder from being saintly and shoot for that possible goal of doing great things for God.

Leadership Too Can Be for Me

> *His master replied, "Well done, good and faithful servant! You have been faithful with a few things; I will put you in charge of many things. Come and share your master's happiness!"*
>
> *—Matthew 25:21 (NIV)*

Just like sainthood, leadership is for us ordinary folks too. We will all get the chance, at some point in our lives, to take the leadership seat and take charge. In fact, we are all called to be leaders in many moments of our lives. We have glamorized leadership positions, and we think that it is just for the extra special people leaving many of us to shy away from leadership roles. We often leave it up for someone else to step up.

However, leadership positions, which are usually perceived as positions of power, authority, and greatness, can potentially draw the wrong kinds of personalities. With such a common perception of leadership, there is the inevitable tendency for the non-humble, the overconfident individuals who think too highly of themselves, the power-hungry, authoritarian, and narcissistic people to pop up and step up to these leadership voids. Our world history has a pantheon of leadership examples with such personalities. Well, hence, another reason why we need to consider the saints' styles as a paragon of leadership. We need the humble, the meek, and even the weak and shy to take up the leadership calling too.

BJ Gonzalvo, Ph.D.

Father Benedict Groeschel used to tell the story of one of his many conversations with Mother Teresa where she told him that God chooses the weakest, the poorest, and the most unlikely instruments to do His work. But in fact, it was through Mother Teresa's humbleness that we recognize her as one of the strongest, most successful, and most effective leaders of the twentieth century. She might never agree with that characterization of her leadership, but looking at where her organization is now and given the way we now view leadership, especially with what research tells us about servant leadership and leading with humility, her leadership was highly effective and truly great. She recognized that leadership is never about the leader. Instead, she knew that it is about the will of God. It is about the organization and its mission. It is about the people.

Learning about the leadership of the saints can help us in our own development, not only in our own spiritual development but in our development as leaders and in how we develop others, our brothers and sisters in Christ, to be leaders. What we get from turning to the saints is an unlikely and different but refreshing model of leadership for us to consider—the kind of leadership that has not only garnered a strong following but has also stood the test of time. It is the kind of leadership that is inherent in our response to a greater calling—the call to holiness.

Amidst our fast-paced world, a time of rapid changes not only of technological and environmental changes, but also of cultural and moral changes, we have an even more pressing reason to look outside of the traditional leadership box. We need to consider leadership models that are timeless and transcendent—models that are proven to be effective no matter the time or the cultural environment. Jorge Mario Bergoglio, the discerning servant of God that he is, must have sensed this need for change when he looked to an eight-hundred-year-old spiritual figure and selected the name Francis to be his papal name. The name he chose is symbolic of things that are happening in the Church now and how Pope Francis is bringing change to the papacy and to the Church.

For the first time in eight hundred years, a pope selects to model after the little poor man of Assisi, Saint Francis—the saint who emphasized humility and servanthood over power and authority. And for the rest of us, the time is ripe to also turn to the saints like Saint Francis of Assisi and countless others, and seek their wisdom. Let us ask them to help us and pray for us. Let us draw strength from them and ask them to help us see, through the lives they lived, some of the most inspirational examples of what leadership should be and how we ought to lead one another closer to Christ.

It is unusual and unlikely for aspiring leaders to look to the saints for leadership examples, but perhaps Pope Francis is onto something here. Now is the time to explore the lives of the saints for the kind of leadership we need today in our society. We need to turn to the examples of the saints not only for proven and effective leadership models, but also for leadership models that will help us and others draw closer to God. Many of the saints were leaders, whether they knew it or not, whether they started a religious order or not. They have earned the right to be recognized as leaders because, even to this day, they continue to influence, to empower, to inspire, to motivate, and to lead. They continue to make sure that they guide us, their younger siblings here on earth, so that we too will someday see the full glory of God.

The lives of the saints might be an unlikely source of leadership wisdom, but sometimes the most effective examples of leadership come from unlikely places. I was surprised with wonder and awe when I started to consider the examples of the saints as models. Consider some of these saints, for example.

Saint Joan of Arc

Who knew that a young teenage girl from a peasant family in a small Medieval village in France would lead an army into victory and eventually be designated the heroine and savior of a nation? When this peasant girl first started having mystical visions and hearing voices of the Divine, no one wanted to take her seriously despite the state of despair their country was in. France, as a nation, was falling apart, and they kept losing battle after battle, but the leaders kept ignoring her. Well, hundreds of years later, we now know a lot about this young village girl. She's France's celebrated national hero, Joan of Arc. Yes, that is right. Who knew that this ordinary teenage girl from a remote village in the countryside would one day be the country's favorite hero?

Don't judge this book by its cover. This young peasant girl was wise beyond her years. She was keenly aware of her nation's situation. France was deep into the Hundred Years War and was suffering one humiliating defeat after another. But this young village girl started a relentless campaign in order to obtain the approval of the townspeople and the leaders. With her unwavering belief that God had chosen her to lead and save France, along with her unrelenting actions in response to that calling, she eventually would lead the French army to victory—many victories. She went from obscurity to being a national hero, and now she is well-recognized as a figure of strong military leadership and as a saint. And who would have known that this kind of strong, courageous leadership would emerge from a very unlikely and very atypical source of leadership?

David

Who would have known that an unknown shepherd boy would be chosen by God to lead his people? He was young and unassuming, and the people did not see anything in him worthy of becoming a leader. But God saw that David was a man after God's own heart, and so He selected him to lead His people. The people did not see that coming, but David was on his way to becoming one of the most important, one of the wisest, and one of the most effective leaders of the Old Testament.

Saint Therese of Lisieux

Who would have known that a young, cloistered nun who had never been anywhere would be destined to be the patron saint of missionaries and a Doctor of the Church? When Saint Therese of Lisieux died after her agonizing struggle with tuberculosis, some of the sisters she was living with were asked to put together some information about her to simply notify the townspeople of her passing. One of the sisters assigned to that task commented that they were not sure what to write about her because she never really did anything. Well, little did they know that this obscure, cloistered nun would later become one of the greatest and most influential saints. It is true: she never went on any missions, never founded a religious order, and never really performed any great deeds. She rarely even went outside of the convent. Everything she did was so ordinary. But somehow, particularly as she approached her death, she knew that her journey and her mission were just about to begin. She died at the young age of twenty-four, but after her death, the love she had for God and others became widely known. She never got to influence a whole lot of people during her life on earth, and yet she had one of the most lasting influences on the Church and on many other souls on their spiritual journey. Her memoir, *Story of a Soul*, published after her death by the order of her prioress, is one of the most widely read Catholic books today. With her very intimate writings, she leads us on a spiritual path that our souls can imitate and follow. She shows us that we do not have to do great things, but we can do small, ordinary things with great humility, obedience, charity, and love. She shows us a sure and safe way to be pleasing to God, and that is through her humble ways, or the "Little Way." And to the surprise of many of her contemporaries, this quiet, humble, cloistered nun had such an important contribution to the theology of the Church. Who would have known that she would one day be recognized and given the title "Doctor of the Church"? She never went on any missions during her lifetime, but now she is considered a Patron of the Missions. Who would have known that a young, sickly nun who rarely got out of the cloisters would inspire many great future missionaries such as Mother Teresa? Saint Therese always had a desire to preach the gospel on all five continents. She never got to leave her cloistered Carmelite convent when she was alive, but today, a hundred years after her death, her life story, her miracles, her inspiration, and also her relic travel around the world, reaching all the continents, proclaiming the love of God!

    In January 2000, I had the privilege to see and venerate the relic of Saint Therese in Seattle, Washington. There must have been over five thousand other people there, Catholics and non-Catholics, Christians and non-Christians, believers and non-believers. Saint James Cathedral was packed, and the line of people getting ready to venerate the relic stretched all the way around the Cathedral block. It was a very moving miracle to witness! There she was, a young, cloistered nun whose earthly journey ended over a century ago. She never got a chance to travel anywhere during her lifetime, yet there she was at one of her stops on her tour around the world, evangelizing and converting people's hearts. She has become a true missionary, leading people closer to God.

Saint Therese never was a leader while alive, but her deep prayer life and her examples—particularly her inner spiritual life and her authentic humble self that shine through her writings—have influenced and continue to influence many people, including some of the saints, such as Mother Teresa, Edith Stein, and Faustina, to live lives that are fully centered on Christ. Her discerning conversations with God, her quiet acts of love, and her humble little ways make up the kind of quiet leadership we need, especially in today's noisy and ego-driven world—or as Susan Cain said in the title of her book, "in a world that can't stop talking."

CHANGING OUR VIEW OF LEADERSHIP

*A leader is one who knows the way,
goes the way, and shows the way.*

—John C. Maxwell

This book is not meant to be just another leadership book that belongs on the business or the leadership shelf of a bookstore. It is not just another book that wants to offer another leadership theory or definition. The time is now ripe for a different view of leadership, and what this book wishes to offer are some inspirations and examples from some of the familiar and well-loved figures of the Catholic Church on leadership, for they have led in a variety of meaningful ways.

Leadership, as many scholars and theorists have conveyed, is one of those familiar concepts yet very hard to pinpoint and define. We are all called to be leaders, and many will hear that call. But before we respond to that call, one of the first things we need to understand is that we need to know what it means to be a leader. We do not need leaders for the sake of having leaders. We do not need leaders who do not have a clear understanding of what leadership is. We do not need misguided leaders who are supposed to be guiding the rest of us. We need leaders who understand what it means to be a leader. We need leaders who understand that the call to lead is part and parcel of God's call to holiness.

Leadership is not about building a following. Many of the saints never intentionally set out to be leaders nor did they attempt to garner a large following, but little did they know that they themselves, through their character, virtues, and faith, personified what effective leadership looks like. Many of them did not start out knowing they were going to be founders of large global organizations nor did they start out knowing they would be saints; but in their response to the call of God and in their constant striving for sanctity, they turned out to be saints and leaders—very well-revered saints and leaders. They did not seek out leadership positions nor did they did seek out greatness but through their actions, their humility, and their service, it was greatness that found them. They led by example, and they led with authenticity, humility, faith, and love. Some of them founded some of the biggest and oldest global institutions that are still flourishing today—The Missionaries of Charity founded by Blessed Mother Teresa, the Franciscans by Saint Francis, the Jesuits by Saint Ignatius, the Dominicans by Saint Dominic, and the Salesians by Saint John Bosco—just to name a few. They were first and foremost seeking the kingdom of God. They were not intending to establish such large organizations. I don't think that they had envisioned being leaders with a large following. Saint Francis even taught it is best for his friars to avoid leadership positions to preserve their very humble positions as servants of God. However, when we closely examine the lives of the saints and the things they have done, we will see that they are leaders who stepped up to face the challenges, they solved the problems before them, they changed people's lives, they led others in very profound ways, and they have earned their followers' trust.

They were first responding to the call to serve God and His people. Leadership guru Robert K. Greenleaf, who coined the phrase "servant leadership" in his 1970 essay, said that "servant leaders are servants first."[8] The saints, in so many ways, were servant leaders. Servant leadership was a role that came naturally to the saints because they had a genuine desire to serve God and His people. And whether they knew it or not, they were servants who became leaders who led others and, in turn, had a lasting impact on people's lives and on the world.

> *Here is a trustworthy saying: Whoever aspires to be a leader desires a noble task*
>
> *—Timothy 3:1*

Do You Want to Be a Leader?

Perhaps it is worth exploring how we now view leadership. If you go around asking people if they want to be leaders, the majority of the answers might be unconfident-sounding no's. Some of that hesitation is mainly due to our perception of leadership as a role that is reserved not for us, personally, but for the person next to us or for the extraordinary and the elite. Many of us might think that leadership is not for us and that positions of leadership should find us versus us trying to seek and pursue leadership. Some might find being a leader to be too intimidating and think that leadership is a role for someone responsible for something so grandiose. Leadership might be narrowly seen as something only for CEOs, generals, presidents, pastors, etc.

If that is the case, what I wish to propose in this book is that we reconsider and reimagine what leadership is. We should not be intimidated. Leadership does not have to be about being extraordinary. It does not have to be about changing the world. Leadership can simply be about positively and genuinely

---

[8] Greenleaf, R. (1991). *The Servant as Leader* (Rev. ed.). Indianapolis, IN: Robert K. Greenleaf Center.

impacting someone's world in small ordinary ways—even if it is just one person. We do not have to reserve our acts of leadership for large groups of people or for special occasions. Leadership can simply be about influence, and it should be within reach of any average individual, every single day. Leadership is about leading one person at a time.

> *Not all of us can do great things. But we can do small things with great love.*
>
> —Mother Teresa

Leadership does not have to be for some monumental task. Leadership opportunities present themselves to us every day, every minute, even in the most ordinary moments. We have to reconsider our perspective on leadership because once we view leadership in this way, in a more bite-sized and demystified way, it will not be hard to see that the call to leadership is everywhere and that it can emerge from anywhere. We can begin to see that the saints, no matter how ordinary their response was to their calling, were great leaders and that they had a lot of leadership wisdom from which we can learn. We can begin to realize that as we follow the footsteps of Christ—our ultimate leader who showed us the way, the truth, and the life—that we too are also called to be leaders.

BJ Gonzalvo, Ph.D.

Leadership Crisis

It does not take much looking around to notice that there is a widespread leadership crisis. In his book *True North*,[9] Harvard Business professor Bill George states that:

> *An enormous vacuum in leadership exists today—in business, politics, government, education, religion, and non-profit organizations. Yet there is no shortage of people with the capacity for leadership. The problem is we have a wrongheaded notion of what constitutes a leader, driven by an obsession with leaders at the top. That misguided stand often results in the wrong people attaining critical leadership roles.*

We have seen organizations experience one crisis after another. We have seen one leadership failure after another. In a research study highlighted by the World Economic Forum in 2015, 86 percent of the survey respondents agreed that we do have a leadership crisis today.[10] People are afraid to step up to the leadership plate. There seems to be a general feeling of disempowerment, and we tend to think that leadership is not for us and we tend to rely on someone else to step up. And when one of us needs to step up to the leadership plate, we don't have a good leadership template out there to follow, so we end up not knowing how to lead.

So, in this shortage of good models of leadership to follow, it is my delight to point out that there are proven and underexplored

---

[9] Bill George, *True North: Discover Your Authentic Leadership* (San Francisco: Jossey-Bass, 2007).

[10] World Economic Forum. "Top Ten Trends of 2015." Accessed from http://reports.weforum.org/outlook-global-agenda-2015/top-10-trends-of-2015/ on May 1, 2017.

leadership models out there already. We do have some of the best, proven, and timeless models of leadership out there in the lives of the saints. These saints understood what leadership is, and they knew what they had to do to lead. And just like how we have a saint for each day of the year, we have a saint for every call to leadership. We don't have to look far for leadership examples to follow.

For those called to some kind of military leadership—there is Saint Joan of Arc or Saint Ignatius.

For those called to nonprofit leadership—there is Mother Teresa or Saint Francis of Assisi.

For political leadership—there is Saint Thomas More.

For education—there is Saint Ignatius or Saint John Bosco.

For leading our families—there is Saint Joseph or Mother Mary.

If we just look closely with an open heart and an open mind, and if we even pray to them for their assistance, we might just discover for ourselves some of the most effective models of leadership that we need not only in our personal lives but in our larger society today.

Need for Strong Leadership Today

If you follow some of the leading authors and thinkers on leadership, you'll notice that there are definite signs all around us that we are experiencing a leadership crisis. Even if you don't follow leadership studies, just turn on the TV and watch the news. Just scroll down your social media newsfeed and you're likely to run into some news about another leadership scandal or another leadership failure. It is happening too often. We seem to struggle to get the right leaders to emerge. And when we find leaders to follow, they seem to end up disappointing us. Despite the volumes of research that we have done on leadership, despite all the articles and blogs about leadership, despite the number of people talking about leadership, despite how much more we know about leadership, we still continue to get bad leadership. It seems that no matter how many coaching, training, and leadership development programs are available out there today in our schools, in our communities, and in our organizations, there still persists a leadership crisis and talent gap for leadership roles.

> *Then I heard the voice of the Lord saying, "Whom shall I send and who will go for us?"*
>
> *—Isaiah 6:8*

We all have probably witnessed or have been a part of failed leadership, whether in corporate settings or even in our family or church communities. We have an idea of how devastating the results of bad leadership can be. And yet, we carry on. We continuously search for proven and effective leadership models. We search for leaders who are not only able to lead us but who can also ensure that the path we, the followers, are on is a path that is morally and ethically righteous. Today, especially, where things have become more complex, more diverse, more technological, and, at times, morally ambiguous, we are in desperate need of a model of leadership that works, a model that we can trust and rely on.

We need authentic leaders, true leaders who can lead us on a path that we can follow with confidence and conviction.

We need humble leaders, not arrogant leaders who are driven primarily by lust for power over others. We need their humility to ensure their followers know that each and every one of them is important and that each and every one of them is made in the image of God.

We need leaders with character. We seem to have forgotten

about the importance of character. Just like what Robert L. Vernon highlighted in his book, character is the foundation of good leadership,[11] yet we forget to start with character when searching for and developing our leaders. As we have seen in numerous debacles, leaders do not fail for lack of technical competence. They don't fail for lack of quality education. Many of the leaders that make it to the top are often highly educated and highly skilled. However, leaders fail not because of lack of skill or technical competence but because of lack of character. Many of the leadership training courses focus on skills, talent, and abilities but very little on character. We've placed a lot of emphasis on the hard skills but we need to shift our focus on developing soft skills, most especially character.

We need godly leaders, men and women who can lead us in the ways of God. Men and women who seek the ways of the Lord. They are leaders who can help us respond to our own callings to be holy. We don't want leadership that will detract us away from God's ways and God's call. We need leaders who are strong in their ethics, morals, and values. Great leaders will lead others around them to greatness—to holiness.

> *Select capable men from all the people, men who fear God, trustworthy men who hate dishonest gain, and appoint them as officials over thousands, hundreds, fifties, and tens.*
>
> *—Exodus 18:21*

---

[11] Robert Vernon, *Character: The Foundation of Leadership* (Pointman Leadership Institute, 2009).

BJ Gonzalvo, Ph.D.

Revisit the Good Book

As we continue to search for good models of leadership, we would be remiss if we forget to look back to see what the wisdom of the ancients can offer us, living in modern times. Let us revisit some of the foundational and timeless wisdom of our faith found in the good book, the Bible. Let us look, for instance, at the book of Proverbs. "How much better to get wisdom rather than gold, to get insight rather than silver" (Proverbs 16:16). The Book of Proverbs has biblical wisdom that gives us essential and enduring lessons about human values, moral behavior, the meaning of life, and, if you read between the lines, there is some valuable wisdom that is directly applicable to leadership. The theme of the Book of Proverbs calls us to some of the true essence of being godly and to some of the most fundamental wisdom that men need today in order to know what God calls us to do and how God calls us to live. For leaders seeking wisdom, the Book of Proverbs is a practical place to start, for it has done a thorough philosophical analysis of human conduct and provides us with a template full of wise instructions for how to live. "In their hearts humans plan their course, but the Lord establishes their steps" (Proverbs 16:9). "Seek first God's wisdom. And seeking God's wisdom first starts with the fear of the Lord and submitting to His will. Leaders seeking wisdom must first start with submitting to God, seeking His wisdom, and discerning His will. "The fear of God is the beginning of wisdom" (Proverbs 9:10). "The fear of the Lord is a fountain of life" (Proverbs 14:27). As a leader, dedicate everything you plan to do to God and He will guide you. "Commit your work to the Lord, and He will establish your plans" (Proverbs 16:3).

Revisit the Wisdom of the Saints

There really is no need to go far and wide searching for leadership models to emulate. You really do not have to look any further than the names of the local parishes around you. Look into the saint your parish church is named after. Get to know the life of your parish's patron saint, and what you will likely find is a treasure trove of wisdom. Exploring the lives of the saints can give us a fresh perspective on leadership for our modern lives. The saints are no longer with us to physically lead us or personally show us leadership, but their examples and lessons for us are timeless and continue to be very applicable. Just like how you have a CEO set his or her vision and drive the company to success, we too have the saints sharing with us their vision and their vision of God's love for us. They are driving us and inspiring us to live holy lives and leading us to the path that deepens our relationship with God. The saints are our older brothers and sisters who have gone before us, yet their lessons and their wisdom remain with us so that they can illuminate for us the way to Christ. Their visions and their wisdom can be found in various places, such as in their writings or in the writings about them, in stories about them, and in the prayers and songs they have taught us. They have been made available to us. Even if they are from many generations past, thanks to them and their followers, we have information now to help us emulate their work.

Thanks to Saint Bonaventure, for example, who wrote about the life of Saint Francis of Assisi—an inspiring book that is considered the official biography of Saint Francis—many of us are familiar with the wonderful works of Saint Francis, and we have the details that can inspire us to do the same. Thanks to Saint Ignatius for writing down his *Spiritual Exercises* that we now have a spiritual how-to manual for deepening our spiritual lives and our relationship with God. Thanks to Saint Therese of Lisieux, now recognized as a Doctor of the Church, for taking the time and the effort to share with us in her writings about her intimate spiritual experiences. Because of her, we now have an inspirational way, the little way, to imitate and to help us draw closer to God by humility, simplicity, and a childlike love for God.

> O Little Therese of the Child Jesus, please
> pick for me a rose from the heavenly gardens
> and send it to me as a message of love.
> O Little Flower of Jesus, ask
> God to grant the favors
> I now place with confidence in your hands.
> Saint Therese, help me to always
> believe as you did in
> God's great love for me, so that I might
> imitate your "Little Way" each day.
> Amen.
>
> —Novena Rose Prayer to Saint Therese

LIKE THE SAINTS

You and I belong to Christ's family, for "He Himself has chosen us before the foundation of the world, to be saints, to be blameless in His sight, for love of Him, having predestined us to be His adopted children through Jesus Christ, according to the purpose of His Will." We have been chosen gratuitously by Our Lord. His choice of us sets us a clear goal. Our goal is personal sanctity, as Saint Paul insistently reminds us, haec est voluntas Dei: sanctificatio vestra, "this is the Will of God: your sanctification." Let us not forget, then, that we are in our Master's sheepfold in order to achieve that goal.

—Homily given by Saint Josemaria Escriva, March 11, 1960

There are many ways to define leadership, and there might never really be a consensus on what leadership is, but we can all agree that Jesus Christ was a leader. Jesus Christ was a leader in so many ways, and He has had the greatest influence in world history. He showed all his followers the way, the truth, and the life. He led by His words. He led by example. And as followers of Christ, we are all called to follow His leadership. We are all called to lead like Christ did. The call to lead is inherent in our calling to follow Jesus Christ.

So again, as I pointed out earlier, you and I, as followers of Christ, are called to be leaders. Yes, you and I, in our own ordinary and average ways, are called to be leaders. You probably have heard many contemporary authors on leadership say, "Anyone can lead." That might sound cliché and too proverbial, but leadership is indeed a skill and an opportunity that is available to each one of us. By virtue of who we are—our true, authentic, and value-driven selves—we all have the calling to lead. It does not mean that we have to have a formal title, hold an office, or be a CEO or an elected president or something. We do, as a society, have the tendency to celebrate the high-profile leaders, but leadership does not necessarily mean that we have to be a celebrated high-profile leader. We do not have to be a leader with some prestigious official title or some position of authority. Not everyone is called to such leadership positions, but each and every one of us is called to exercise leadership.

We all have that calling. We are all called to make a difference. Some of the thought leaders, such as Stephen Covey, said that to lead is our birthright. The call to lead is a universal call from above that is for everyone to hear.

A Follower and a Leader

In our calling as Christians to follow Christ, our leader, an important but overlooked part of that call is the call to lead others as Christ did. It is apparent that as followers of Christ, we are called to be followers, but we seem to have dichotomized and polarized the two roles of follower and leader. We seem to have gotten stuck conceptually separating followers from leaders. Leaders do not have to be solely leaders. They are also followers.

The same goes for followers. Followers do not have to be solely followers; they are also leaders. Good followers make good leaders. We must first be good followers before we become good leaders. As Christians, we must first be good followers of Christ before we become good leaders.

It might get chaotic if everyone started acting as a leader so we have to be careful not to misunderstand what leadership is and have everyone act presidential. Organizations have a natural tendency to have leadership, so there has to be someone in charge. There has to be someone acting as a leader to lead others. Even though we are all called to be leaders, we cannot all act like leaders. Leadership is a calling from God that must be carefully discerned. It also does not mean that being a leader means that you are above your followers.

Followers are also called to be leaders. Sooner or later, followers will also need to step up and lead their fellow followers. Followers must not be disempowered and refrain from becoming leaders. Leaders need their followers to be unceasingly engaged in the mission of the group, and leaders must learn how to draw the best out of their followers.

Followers need the leaders, but leaders also need their followers in so many ways. Leaders are great individuals, but they will not know it all, and we need to steer away from that thinking. We cannot expect our leaders to know it all. Leaders must not play the role like they know it all.

Followers also have talents, gifts, and expertise, and they too should be empowered to lead right from where they are as followers. Leaders who recognize the value of their followers will know how to be good followers themselves. Followers who recognize the value they bring to the mission of the organization will know how to be leaders in their own ways.

Followers of Christ responding to the call to lead will realize that the concept of leadership is fundamentally different from how society currently defines leadership. Over the years, we seem to have misconstrued leadership. As we respond to the call to lead, we need to take some time to look at what leadership is, what it has become, and what it should look like. We need to examine our own understanding of what leadership is. We need to see how history has shaped the meaning of leadership and how we now interpret it.

As Christian leaders, we need to have examples of leadership that are aligned to the teachings of Christ. We look at the lives of the Catholic saints because they are the best examples that fully demonstrate for us what leadership should be. They are saints canonized by the Catholic Church, recognized, identified, and made official by Church authorities because they truly and authentically followed Christ and lived exceptionally holy lives. They responded to the call of Christ to follow Him, and, in following Christ, these saints themselves turned out to be great leaders themselves. They responded to the call to follow Christ, and through their behaviors and the way they lived their lives, they themselves inspired others and gained their own following; they led countless others to live meaningful and God-centered lives. It is through their examples, their actions, their words, and the way they lived their lives that we are provided a template for how we ourselves ought to live, love, and lead.

And though they are canonized and recognized by the Church to be saints, let us not forget that these saints were also once ordinary people who walked this earth and were just like us, with the same earthly circumstances and challenges. They too lived in this world; some were businessmen, teachers, parents, students, priests, brothers, sisters, etc., but they responded to God's calling in exceptional ways. These saintly figures exemplified how to follow Christ and live the gospel. And by following Christ, they too were exuding leadership qualities that others, including us facing twenty-first-century problems and issues, can still follow.

Have an Encounter

There is no doubt that our conceptualization of leadership has changed over the years, but there really is no need to look for new leadership models or try to reinvent what leadership is. We just have to revisit the timeless wisdom that has already been laid out for us by the Bible as well as in the lives of the saints and see how we can apply them to our own circumstances. We just need to shine a light on their lives and highlight their leadership examples, which we can use as models for our own leadership aspirations.

Regardless of where you are in your life or career, you can find inspiration in the lives of the saints to keep you moving forward in the right direction. Whether you are a student, a teacher, a parent, a worker, a manager, a team leader, a boss, or a team member, you are called to make a difference, and you have in you the potential to lead. Being a leader is not a predetermined or an exclusive, fixed, and innate capability that is available only to a select few. We all have the potential as well as the opportunity to lead because, as social beings, we are always surrounded by others. Human beings are ultimately social and interdependent. Each one of us has a sphere of influence (see 2 Corinthians 10:15). Aristotle, the great philosopher, said that it is our natural inclination as human beings to be part of a community. It is natural for us to want to belong to a community.[12] Many anthropologists and social scientists will argue that the survival of our species has depended on our ability to form communities. We need one another. Even the latest research in sociology suggests that our need to connect with people is even more fundamental than our need for food and shelter.[13] And so as we get together and build communities, the opportunity to lead others is available to each one of us. We all

---

[12] Aristotle, trans. 1957. *Politics*. I.2.1252b27–30
[13] Matthew D. Lieberman, *Social: Why Our Brains Are Wired to Connect* (Crown, 2013).

have the opportunity to impact each other's lives. John C. Maxwell nicely summed up what leadership essentially is: "Leadership is influence, nothing more, nothing less."[14] And so if leadership is influence, then all of us have that potential to influence others. Our actions, our words, our deeds, and our beliefs all have the potential to influence others.

The saints changed the lives not only of the people they met but also of those who later heard of their exploits. I encourage you to know their stories in further detail because their stories truly have the power to touch lives. And in addition to simply learning about their examples, I also urge you to seek their intercession and to ask them to pray for us, that they may guide us and show us; and that they may illuminate the path for us, the path that leads us closer to God so that we too can lead saintly lives as well as lead others onto this path. And as Father Benedict Groeschel called for in one of his many books, "Let us pray with the saints, pray with them in their own words, and have an encounter with the living God just like they did."

Why the Saints?

Think of some of the oldest organizations still around today. One of the oldest still in operation, General Electric, was incorporated just over a hundred years ago in 1889. The Boy Scouts was founded in 1908. McDonald's Restaurant, the world's largest restaurant chain, was founded in 1940. Microsoft was founded in 1974. According to a 2013 *Forbes* article, the lifespan

---

[14] John C. Maxwell, *Developing the Leader Within You* (Thomas Nelson Inc, 1993).

Lessons in Leadership from the Saints

of a typical company in this day and age is about fifteen years.[15] One of the criterion researchers argued before was that one true measure of successful leadership is sustainability and survival.[16] Sometimes we measure leaders by how long the organizations they led endured. And there's not a lot of organizations that have endured for hundreds of years. For an organization to have been around for hundreds of years and still continue to flourish and still continue to make an impact on society, there has to be something profoundly special going on. The leadership in that organization must have done something extraordinary.

These corporate giants are some of the oldest, but they are young compared to some of the religious orders we know today. The Franciscans and the Dominicans are groups founded in the thirteenth century, hundreds of years ago, and are still going strong to this day. The Jesuits, the religious order where Pope Francis comes from, was founded in the 1500s by Saint Ignatius and is also still continuing to flourish to this day. The group that Mother Teresa founded, the Missionaries of Charity, one of the youngest religious orders, has only been around since 1950, but it's still going strong and was, in fact, one of the fastest orders to grow. Ten years after her passing in 1997, the group grew dramatically to over five thousand brothers and sisters with operations in over one hundred and twenty countries. It is a community that is still growing and continually attracting a large following to this day.

And for someone interested in studying organizations like myself, I am curious about such phenomenon. So what is it about these long-established groups that make them tick? What makes them tick now, and what made them tick in the beginning?

Well, one key aspect of that enduring success is the leadership

---

[15] David K. Williams, "Staying in Business Forever: How to Create a 100-Year Company." (April 10, 2013). Accessed from Forbes.com on July 16, 2016.

[16] Michael T. Hannan and John Freeman, "The Population Ecology of Organizations," *American Journal of Sociology*, (March 1977, 929–964).

these organizations had—leadership right from the start with their founders and their vision, followed by the leadership throughout the centuries that kept the same vision, carried out their work and kept the torchlight burning.

And what did the leaders and the founders do to drive their organizations to success? What attracted the initial members to the founder? And even today, centuries after their organizations were founded, what draws new members? What makes people today and throughout all these years continue to follow their principles and their ideals? Just what exactly did these leaders and founders have that sparked their first following? And what keeps that torchlight lit, that spark shining and continuing to shine its light and energize generations of new followers and new leaders through the ages?

Their examples of leadership were something definitely noteworthy for many reasons, but are also remarkable, especially for those interested in organizational studies, simply because of the fact that their organizations and their followers continue to follow their ways, their vision, and their mission, even to this day. That spark that the saints and blessed leaders ignited during their living years continues to flame up hundreds of years later. There are many different theories and stories about leadership nowadays, and we know more about leadership than ever before, but we don't hear enough about the types of leadership demonstrated by these saints. Their leadership is something else.

It wasn't the intentions of the saints to have such large following; I doubt if they had envisioned that the organizations they started would continue to flourish even up to the twenty-first century, but they sure did flourish for a long time. With their leadership, their vision, their charism, and their teachings, we still have the organizations they founded doing great things in our world today. The simple fact that their organizations lasted centuries is evidence enough that there is something about their leadership that is worthy of our pursuit today as we grapple with trying to understand what leadership is and what it should be.

Traditionally, we look up to the saints because they serve as models of the faith and exemplars of how it is to live meaningful Christian lives, but their stories are also full of leadership examples that demonstrate to us ordinary laypeople how we too can also be great leaders like them. We have the saints to imitate and follow because they knew how to imitate and follow Jesus Christ. In the words of Saint Paul, in his various letters found in the New Testament, he encouraged others to imitate him as he is an imitator of Christ. In his letter to the Corinthians, he said: "Follow my example as I followed the example of Christ" (1 Corinthians 11:1). Saints have become imitators of the disciples and of the Lord, and now they too can serve as models for all believers. "You became imitators of us and of the Lord, for you welcomed the message in the midst of severe suffering with the joy given by the Holy Spirit, so that you became a model to all the believers" (1 Thessalonians 1:6–7). We are on the shoulders of spiritual giants, and it is by following the examples they set for us that we, in turn, are setting the examples for others around us. By following their lead, we, in turn, get to lead others—just as Saint Paul and the many saints who followed him—up the same path that brings us all closer to God.

We are blessed to have in our church family the saints. In this church family, we are in communion with the saints who are, as author Scott Hahn calls in his book, *Angels and Saints*, our "older brothers and sisters in Christ." In our communion with the saints, we join them and our fellow Christians in being imitators of Christ, and observe those who conduct themselves according to the model that we have in them (Philippians 3:17). And in Saint Paul's letter to the Hebrews: "Remember your leaders, who spoke the word of God to you. Consider the outcome of their way of life and imitate their faith" (Hebrews 13:7).

Like Mike

When I was teaching Catechism to young teens, I would often use sports analogies as a tool to connect with my audience and deliver my points. Sports analogies have the tendency to activate the brain and help facilitate connections for the audience. And sports and the Christian journey have a lot in common. In sports, we like to model after people who we think are great at what they do. I did that a lot when I was a kid. As a young kid, I would often imagine myself becoming one of the great athletes. I admired the likes of Michael Jordan, Joe Montana, and Ken Griffey, Jr. None of my imaginations even came close to materializing, but it was nice to dream. For some who are talented enough, however, they found a way. I have witnessed in my lifetime this life-long evolutionary process where some of the younger players become like their models as they grew older. I have witnessed that for someone who is aspiring to become an exceptionally good basketball player, he or she might want to study, learn, and model after basketball icons like Michael Jordan, Kobe Bryant, or Lebron James. He or she might even want to pick up books and videos about their personal lives and find out what motivated them to become great basketball players. He or she could watch films and study their moves. I know for my generation, a lot of us watched Michael Jordan's *Come Fly with Me* growing up. A lot of basketball players today grew up watching Michael Jordan and they are now, in so many ways, emulating his gravity-defying moves and his relentless work ethic. They had Michael Jordan to model after when they were growing up and now, they, themselves, have become great players.

It happens a lot in sports. Aspiring athletes can pick specific skills that they want to develop and model after specific players' skillsets. Maybe they would like to work on their long-range shooting like Steph Curry, or maybe their hang time like Michael Jordan, or maybe their passing skills like Magic Johnson. Perhaps they want to combine all these skills into one package to become a well-rounded and versatile basketball player. And besides watching and admiring these basketball superstars, besides having their posters on the wall or having their jerseys on their back, aspiring athletes know that they would also have to be committed to putting in the hours to physically train and practice in order to become as good as their models. Becoming like the great figures is not an easy task. It requires dedication, hard work, and perseverance. But just like their models who have gone before them, it is possible; if there's a will, there is always a way.

Like Francis, Like Pio, Like Teresa

So to translate this phenomenon from sports into spiritual life, for those aspiring to become holy, the aspirant might want to study, learn, and model after the likes of Saint Francis and his humility, Mother Teresa and her compassion, and Padre Pio and his perseverance. One would also have to put in the hours to train and practice to become spiritually strong like the saints. Becoming like the saints that we look up to also requires dedication, hard work, and perseverance.

And as athletes have playbooks and training guides, spiritual seekers have meditational guides and spiritual books to follow. We can implement the spiritual exercises that Saint Ignatius himself practiced over five hundred years ago. These spiritual exercises are used today by many who wish to strengthen their spiritual lives and grow closer to God. We can read Saint Bonaventure's *The Mind Road to God* to help us contemplate and trace the path toward finding God.

So as young, aspiring athletes have heroes to model after, we too have the saints to help us develop into saintly individuals ourselves. Saint Teresa of Avila, for instance, as a child was always fascinated by the saints, especially women martyrs for the faith.

She digressed a bit when she started to chase after superficial things. She started to dress fashionably, use perfumes, and wear vain ornaments. But then as she continued to grow, not only in age but also in her spirituality, she instead turned to the stories of the saints to inspire and motivate her. When she became a young adult faced with the decision to choose a vocation, it was the works of Saint Jerome, one of the early Church Fathers, that led her to choose the religious life.

The saints are not only our models and guides; they serve as intercessors for us, asking that God grant us His grace to strengthen us on our journey toward holiness. We are blessed to have their examples to emulate as we try to figure out how we can respond to God's call. As Mother Angelica of EWTN used to say often, "We are all called to be saints." Saint Paul the Apostle, in his letter to the Corinthians, said, "We are called to be saints."[17] Again, it is a call that reminds us that it is not just for the select few. It is a call for ordinary laypersons, like me and you. It is a call we share with the saints. And though the acts of the saints are incredibly tough to follow, they do provide us with real-life examples that show us that saintliness is not impossible. Their stories are true ones that we can all relate to. We might not live monastic lives or we might not all be living in a convent, but there are many ways, in our own walks of life, that call us to holiness. Let us not forget that many of the saints also lived in very worldly times similar to the worldliness we currently live in. The saints' very human stories tell us that it is possible in our own daily ways to live and lead just like they did—recognizing those God-laden moments and responding willingly and lovingly with faithfulness and holiness. In a time when we are in desperate need of good, exemplary figures to take us to a state where we can better realize our full potential as human beings—as children of God made in His image, called to sanctity and to leadership—we are blessed as a

---

[17] See 1 Corinthians 1:2.

family of God to have the saints, as our older brothers and sisters, lead us and show us the way, not only to leadership but to holiness.

Leadership is Influence

Leadership is influence, nothing more, nothing less.

—John C. Maxwell

Over all these years of trying to understand leadership, we now understand that leadership is a call to influence others. As Christians, leadership is a calling. And each individual human being has the potential to lead and positively influence others. This realization in leadership philosophy is a reflection of where we have been as a society in the last hundred years, including our journey from the industrial age to the information age. The leadership that works for the people of today is different than the domineering power of one person over others. Leadership is not about control. It does not coerce or manipulate. Instead, leadership gets to the hearts and minds of the people. Leadership looks out for the needs of others; it does not dictate and force people to do something against their will. Effective leadership listens and understands the people, their needs, and their values. Effective leaders empower others. Effective leaders inspire. And if you look at the word *inspire*, it means "in spirit." Leadership is inspirational and in tune with the spirit of the people.

The saints have some of the most motivational stories that inspire us to stand up for our beliefs and to follow them in their virtuous ways. Who does not get inspired when hearing of the authentic love of Francis for God and God's creations? Who does not find Mother Teresa's life story of compassion for the people neglected by society inspirational? Who does not find Saint Ignatius's devotion and dedication inspirational? Who doesn't find Saint Teresa of Avila's inner struggles for holiness relatable?

The saints' deeds and actions have inspired so many people to emulate them and to follow in their footsteps because we know that their footsteps surely and evidently led them to holiness and to oneness with Christ. We have a great deal to learn from the saints about being leaders—about how to take up our own cross and follow their lead. These saints were called to follow Christ, our leader. And they responded. They themselves became leaders that we now can follow and imitate. Some of them faced very tough situations, and it might be hard to measure up to what they did. But we can relate to them and draw inspiration from them, because not only did they inspire the immediate members of the groups they founded, but they also inspired other well-known leaders in history who lived years or even centuries after them.

Saint Francis of Assisi, for instance, inspired many in history who themselves became inspiring leaders, such as his contemporary, Saint Clare, who founded the Order of Poor Ladies; Pope John XXIII; Joan of Arc; Galileo; voyager Christopher Columbus; and one of the most inspirational leaders of the twentieth century, Mahatma Gandhi. And now perhaps the most recent well-known leader influenced by Saint Francis, we have Pope Francis, who actually chose his papal name after Saint Francis of Assisi as a signal to the world who he will be emulating.

His birth name was Jorge Mario Bergoglio. But the moment he was elected by his fellow cardinals to be pope, a good Cardinal friend hugged him, kissed him, and said to him, "Don't forget the poor." And so, taking that statement to heart, Jorge Mario Bergoglio went ahead and started his mission as pope dedicated to the poor, modeling after Saint Francis's hallmark love for the poor. His first move as newly elected pope was to choose a papal name that would serve as the symbol for the kind of papacy he intends to fulfill. He chose the name Francis after Saint Francis of Assisi.

And so as bearer of that name, he chose to embrace poverty and to live a simple, humble life, like Saint Francis of Assisi embraced humility and what he affectionately referred to as "lady poverty."

Just a few decades ago, I was blessed to have witnessed another prominent saintly figure who was deeply influenced by Saint Francis of Assisi—Mother Teresa of Calcutta. If you go to a nearby poverty-stricken neighborhood soup kitchen, it is very likely that you'll run into the group that she inspired: the Missionaries of Charity. You can detect Saint Francis's influence in Mother Teresa's humility, her spirituality, and her life's devotion to serving the poor. It is well-documented that one of her favorite prayers is the beautiful prayer that has been traditionally attributed to Saint Francis, *the Peace Prayer*:

> *Lord, make me an instrument of Thy peace.*
> *Where there is hatred, let me sow love;*
> *Where there is injury, pardon;*
> *Where there is doubt, faith;*
> *Where there is despair, hope;*
> *Where there is darkness, light;*
> *Where there is sadness, joy.*
> *O divine Master, grant that I may not so much seek*
> *To be consoled as to console,*
> *To be understood as to understand,*
> *To be loved as to love;*
> *For it is in giving that we receive;*
> *It is in pardoning that we are pardoned;*
> *It is in dying to self that we are born to eternal life.*

John C. Maxwell, one of the leading authorities on the topic of leadership today, emphasized in many of his works the point that "the true measure of leadership is influence, nothing more, nothing less." Our power to influence others is a power that we often underestimate as human beings. Each one of us have this power to influence others. If leadership is influence, as many of the leadership experts say, we all have that power to influence.

What better way to demonstrate how to influence as a leader than to look to the leadership of Mother Teresa, Saint Francis, Pope Francis, and the many saints who have influenced us. There can never be leadership without influence, and these luminaries of our Church have had a lasting influence that spans generations and even centuries. People seek their influence. People have sought them so that they can follow them and imitate their deeds and their virtues. People seek to follow them because they know that the saints' ways are proven ways of living a holy life and getting closer to God. The saints understood that their primary purpose as leaders was to lead, to show others the way, to inspire, and to influence their fellow brothers and sisters in Christ toward the desired outcome. That desired outcome is for us to know God's love, for us to be closer to God, and for us to be one with God in eternity.

*The goal of our life is to live with God forever.
God, who loves us, gave us life.
Our own response of love allows God's life
to flow into us without limit.
All the things in this world are gifts from God,
Presented to us so that we can
know God more easily
and make a return of love more readily.
As a result, we appreciate and
use all these gifts of God
insofar as they help us to develop
as loving persons.
But if any of these gifts become
the center of our lives,
they displace God
and so hinder our growth toward our goal.
In everyday life, then, we must
hold ourselves in balance
before all of these created gifts
insofar as we have a choice
and are not bound by some obligation.
We should not fix our desires on health or sickness,
wealth or poverty, success or failure,
a long life or a short one.
For everything has the potential
of calling forth in us
a deeper response to our life in God.
Our only desire and our one choice should be this:
I want and I choose what better leads
to God's deepening His life in me.*

*—Saint Ignatius's Spiritual Exercises:
The First Principle and Foundation*

LEADERSHIP THROUGH THE YEARS

If you were asked to bring to mind a leader, who or what is the usual image that comes to mind? Is that person a president? A military general? Perhaps a successful CEO? Maybe even your own boss? A sports figure, maybe?

How about a saint? And why not a saint? How likely are you to bring to mind a saint, any saint, as a leader? Not too many of us are likely to conjure up in our heads a saint as a leader. Leadership studies rarely highlight the examples of the saints when talking about leaders. It is unlikely that you'll see a saint on the cover of a business magazine or even on the pages of a leadership textbook. Sadly, mainstream thinking just doesn't see the saints fit the traditional leadership box. We tend to brush them off when we try to picture a leader. So if you ask someone to think of a leader today, it might be unlikely to have names like Saint Francis, Saint Dominic, Saint Ignatius, Saint Therese, or Mother Teresa come up. We seldom see or hear a saint's name come up as an example of leadership. We have a common image of what a leadership template looks like—probably someone who stands with confidence, someone who is strong, tall, well-groomed, and attractive. The saints who are familiar to many of us are probably portrayed as the exact opposite of that image—some dressed in raggedy beggar clothes and worn-out sandals, and were balding, slouched, small in stature, and scruffy-looking.

Though the saints might not necessarily fit the leadership roles description, they are actually some of the most admirable leaders who have made their marks on this earth; and they have profoundly influenced and inspired millions of followers around the world for many centuries now. Mother Teresa, for example—one of the more recent saintly figures to walk this earth and one that I was blessed enough to have witnessed in action—was a humble and simple lady. She was less than five feet in stature and wore the same simple garment every day, and can be seen as one of the greatest leaders of our time. She has influenced so many people around the world and has been the subject of many books, biographies, and documentaries. She led one of the largest international organizations, which started with only twelve sisters, and grew that to over four thousand members serving in one hundred and twenty-three countries by the time of her death in 1997. Several years after her passing, the Missionaries of Charity continue to thrive and do great things around the world, including caring for the poor, the sick, and the homeless, and running orphanages, soup kitchens, counseling programs, and schools.

Mother Teresa had such a lasting influence that the group she founded just a little over sixty years ago continues to gain a strong following around the world. More people, particularly the young of today, continue to be drawn to the Missionaries of Charity, following Mother Teresa's footsteps as they respond to God's call for them, giving up their belongings and leaving the comfort of their homes so that they can serve the poorest of the poor.

If leadership is about positive influence, as proposed by one of the foremost authorities on the topic of leadership, John C. Maxwell,[18] then there is no doubt that Mother Teresa and these other saints are leaders because they have influenced and continue

---

[18] John C. Maxwell, *Developing the Leader Within You* (Thomas Nelson, 2005).

to influence and inspire a great number of people. They are leaders in the sense that they responded to their calling in life, stood up to face the challenges before them, and seized the opportunity to make a difference in the world and in the lives of many people. They responded to the call of Christ to follow Him, to rebuild His church, and to extend Christ's message of hope and love to others.

Believe it or not, despite our shortcomings and sinfulness, we too are called every day, just like the saints were, to follow Christ and to make a difference. And as members of the Catholic Church family, we have the saints as our older brothers and sisters who have gone before us and who are now watching over us. Let us turn to the saints, look at their lives, and open our eyes and our hearts so that we can see what lessons in leadership they can offer us as we continue our journey in life with one another as brothers and sisters in Christ. Let us use the influence of the saints to influence one another. We do not have to be great leaders doing great things to have an influence, but we can, as Mother Teresa and Saint Therese of Lisieux used to say, do small things with great love. Sometimes, and sometimes unbeknownst to us, our small acts of love have the greatest influence on others.

How Leadership Got Here

If we are all called to be leaders, it is one necessary and important step to ensure that we have a good understanding of what leadership is. We might also have to try and know how we have come to our current view of what leadership is. To understand our calling as leaders, we have to dispel our misconceptions of what leadership is. If we are called to follow Christ, including His leadership, we need to try to understand what leadership is and what makes a leader. If you are not a leader yet, sooner or later, there will be someone else who will notice your actions and your potential to lead. You will then be called to step up and lead. And once you are made an official leader, would you then have a leadership template to model after? Would that leadership template conflict with your Christian calling?

And even if we are not yet called to lead in a formal way, as Christians who are shown *the way*, we should heed the call to step up, to lead, and to show *the way* to others. The time is now to find that leadership template that we can follow and use for inspiration. We turn to the saints, for they have exemplified some of the best leadership principles and models out there. But first, let's take the time to understand what leadership means, what leadership is, how we view leadership, its traditional meaning or meanings (plural, because leadership means different things to different people), its evolution over time, and what it means for us to have the saints as leaders. For a more complete picture of what leadership is, let's do a quick review of the history of leadership. Looking at how we have viewed leadership over the years will give us a sense for how we, as a society, have come a long way in this respect. Throughout history, we have seen many different kinds of leadership styles and many kinds of leaders—some good ones and, unfortunately, some downright horrible ones. We have seen malevolent and benevolent leaders. We have seen leaders who can be righteous philosopher kings, just like Roman Emperor Marcus Aurelius, hailed as one of the noblest emperors of ancient history; but on the other hand, we have also seen leaders in history who have been straight-up dictators with immoral and very evil intentions. And unfortunately, they are still classified as leaders.

In leadership studies, we have been, for a long time now, trying to understand what leaders are, what makes them, why we follow them, and how someone can become a leader. We certainly now know more about leadership, but the more we learn, the more we realize how much more elusive it really is. Leadership discussions date back to the days of the early Greeks and even ancient Egyptian and Chinese societies. Homer, Plato, Aristotle,

Confucius, and other thinkers of the past have all discussed the topic of leadership, and they have all known about the importance of leadership in society.

Over time, particularly in recent years, leadership discussions got more scholarly. Many of our current leadership theories began to emerge around the same time we started to learn fascinating things about psychology and human behavior in the early 1900s—thanks to Sigmund Freud, B.F. Skinner, Erick Erickson, and other figures that you probably studied in Psychology 101. In the last fifty years alone, there have been over a thousand studies that have attempted to determine the leadership styles, traits, and characteristics of a great leader, but none have captured the definitive profile. No one theory is adequate to tell the whole story about leadership. With all the countless books, articles, research studies, and discussions about leadership, it still remains a concept that is familiar to many people whose true nature continues to be elusive. Sometimes, we just have to humbly accept that leadership is not an easy concept to grasp. And when it comes to choosing our leaders and in striving to be a leader, we have to be mindful that prudence is required to avoid bad leadership but also to enhance the chances of having great leaders in our society.

Wrong Models of Leadership

As a society, we have always needed leadership. Whether it is in the church, in our communities, in government, in the military, in ancient tribes, or in any organization, the need for leadership is a constant. However, we know that not all leaders are equal. Not every person who steps up to the leadership plate sees and treats leadership the same way.

As we've seen throughout history, leadership positions are vulnerable to attracting the wrong individuals. Too often, we get individuals aspiring for and stepping up to leadership positions who are just hungry for control and power. They can be proud, arrogant, self-centered, egotistical, and even narcissistic.

Narcissistic individuals tend to find ways that allow them to slide into leadership positions. They tend to just somehow emerge. In fact, researchers from Ohio State University found that narcissistic people are the ones likely to emerge and take control of leaderless groups.[19] Some of these narcissist individuals might actually make good leaders, but we have to be wary of such individuals. We cannot simply assume that just because of their knack to step up and slide into leadership positions that they would make more effective leaders than others. Narcissist individuals crave power and they seek it. They are egotistical. They often seek the admiration of others. They will often do whatever it takes to attain leadership positions. They view these leadership positions as a means to satisfy their own selfish cravings. They will try to be charming and act extroverted as they take over leadership groups. And followers get blinded and deceived by these leaders.

In some ways, our view of leadership and our models of leadership have misguided us and, in many cases, have failed us in what we expect from our leaders. Some of the ways we view leadership have also misguided aspiring leaders, thus rendering them ineffective. So to help understand what leadership is, let's look at what some of the misconceptions are and what leadership is not.

For one, leadership is not the same thing as management. This is one of the first things business schools teach about leadership. Leadership and management go hand-in-hand, but they are not one and the same. Equating leadership with management is one of the most common myths about leadership. Leadership

---

[19] Brunell, A.B., Gentry, W.A., Campbell, W.K., Hoffman, B.J., Kuhnert, K.W., & Demarree, K.G., "Leader Emergence: The Case of the Narcissistic Leader," *Society for Personality and Social Psychology* (Dec. 2008), 1663–1676.

is not managing people; instead, leadership is motivating and influencing people. One way to differentiate the two is by thinking of it this way: leaders have followers while managers have workers. And in our knowledge economy where there is the pervasive rise of the knowledge workers, management guru Peter Drucker observed that we can no longer manage knowledge workers.[20] Today's workers don't need managers. Instead, they need leaders who will motivate and influence them so that they perform at their full potential.

Leadership should not be about having authority or power over people. The Bible taught us this a long time ago: "Not domineering over those in your charge" (Peter 5:3). Leadership is not about overpowering others, but instead, it is about empowering others.

Leadership is not about being popular. It is not about the external physical appearance. It is not about good looks or good hair or a fit body. It is not about who is taller or has a more commanding presence, even though that is a common hidden bias that people tend to have. Leadership is about what is on the inside of the person.

How we select leaders should not be based on external physical appearance, but many of us might not be aware that we do have this implicit bias, this tendency to appoint leaders based on the way they look, the way they dress, or the way they stand. For instance, several research studies have shown that we have the tendency to evaluate leadership abilities based on the facial features, such as facial attraction and facial maturity. Our bias is toward selecting leaders who look older and more mature without necessarily considering their actual level of maturity.

We also have the tendency to evaluate leadership abilities based on height. It is a well-known phenomenon that many of the leaders we put in position are head and shoulders above

---

[20] Peter F. Drucker, "Knowledge Worker Productivity: The Biggest Challenge," *California Management Review, Vol.41, No.2* (1999), 79–94.

others. About two-thirds of presidential candidates are taller than average, and in two-thirds of all US presidential elections, the taller candidate won. If you look at some of the global leaders, they tend to be taller than the average height in their respective countries. In the corporate world, many of the Fortune 500 CEOs seem to be taller than average. In fact, only 4 percent of Americans are over the height of six foot two, and yet, as Malcolm Gladwell pointed out in his book *Blink,* over 30 percent of CEOs are taller than that. This quantified piece of information indicates that there is the convincing possibility that we, collectively, have the tendency beneath our consciousness to put leaders into position based on physical characteristics. There is this apparent tendency for someone's height to be a significant factor in getting selected as a leader. A 2004 research study by Timothy A. Judge of the University of Florida and Daniel M. Cable of the University of North Carolina found that there is indeed a correlation between height and salary.[21] The taller the person, the more money they make. We do have the implicit bias to assign taller people to higher positions, hence higher pay.

We are a very appearance-based culture, and we tend to judge a book by its cover. We do have the tendency to subliminally choose leadership based on external characteristics and physical appearance, leaving us susceptible to losing sight of what is on the inside, what is in people's hearts, and what true leadership is about. We need to be mindful of this bias and look beyond the person's external appearance and physical characteristics when selecting who we follow.

Mother Teresa undoubtedly was a great leader; a book title even referred to her as a "CEO."[22] But her leadership is one that

---

[21] Timothy Judge and Daniel Cable, "The Effect of Physical Height on Workplace Success and Income: Preliminary Test of a Theoretical Model," *Journal of Applied Psychology,* 89 (2004), 428–441.

[22] Ruma Bose & Lou Faust. *Mother Teresa, CEO: Surprising Principles for Practical Leadership* (New York, MJF Books, 2011).

goes against the grain of our conception of leaders. She was barely five feet tall, she looked very fragile and old, and she wore the same plain garment every day. And yet, look at how effective she was as a leader. Look at how much God has blessed her in leading an international organization that grew rapidly. In their book *Gracious Christianity: Living the Love We Possess*, authors Douglas Jacobsen and Rodney J. Sawatsky wrote, "Mother Teresa was far from beautiful in the glamour magazine-sense of the word but she was clearly one of the most attractive people in the world because of her moral beauty and compassion for the poorest of the poor in Calcutta's slum."[23] It was her graciousness and kindness; it was what was in her heart, so pure, so holy, and so full of prayer, that she was able to successfully lead and grow the Missionaries of Charity.

And then there is Saint Francis of Assisi—the Little Poor Man of Assisi. We have all seen a statue or an image of Saint Francis of Assisi. In many of the representations, he's dressed in beggar's clothes and didn't care much for his physical appearance. There is an often-told story of a conversation between Saint Francis and Brother Masseo, one of the original twelve followers of Francis. Brother Masseo was tall, handsome, and considered to be one of the best preachers of the new budding order. One day, Brother Masseo tried to test Francis's humility and so, half-jokingly, he asked Francis:

"Why you? Why are people always after you?"

Saint Francis, curious to know the reason behind the question, replied, "What do you mean, Brother Masseo?"

"I mean, why is everyone running after you? Everywhere we go, why does everyone want to see you or hear you and obey you?

---

[23] Douglas Jacobsen and Rodney J. Sawatsky, *Gracious Christianity: Living the Love We Possess* (Michigan: Baker Academic, 2006), p.18.

You're not a handsome man. You're not a learned man. You're not a nobleman. So why is everybody after you?"

> Upon hearing Brother Masseo's question, Saint Francis rejoiced in humility, lifted up his gaze toward heaven, knelt down, thanked the Lord, and began to address Brother Masseo's question. Saint Francis responded by quoting 1 Corinthians 1:27:
>
> "God chose the foolish things of the world to shame the wise; God chose the weak things of the world to shame the strong." Praise God that I am none of these you described. God chose me for there is no other more sinful and more unworthy. God is showing the path to simplicity and truth and that He does this through such lowly dirt as me.

In a society that is obsessed with beauty, we place such a high value on physical appearance. We have to be aware of this bias and tendency so that we are cautious when we select our leaders. We subconsciously use socially constructed bias and superficial criteria, and that can have a blinding effect on us. Let us not miss the next Saint Francis or Mother Teresa because we got fixated on the seductions of external appearances and not what is genuinely in their hearts.

In the Book of 1 Samuel, when the Israelites were searching for a king to rule over them, God chose David as their king over others, including the people's choice, Saul. Saul, who was handsome, physically dominating, and stood head and shoulders above his countrymen, was the leader that the people wanted. God, however, saw that his heart was not rightly inclined toward Him and so rejected him and chose David instead. In comparison to Saul, David looked young and was not as tall. He just didn't seem to have the physical characteristics that people look for in their leaders. But the Lord saw beyond what was on the outside. The Lord said to Samuel, "Do not look on his appearance or on the height of his stature, because I have rejected him. For the Lord does not see as mortals see; they look on the outward appearance, but the Lord looks on the heart" (1 Samuel 16:7). God saw that David was a man after God's heart who would do the will of God (Acts 13:22).

Better Understanding of Leadership

How should we select our next leaders? What exactly is this thing we call leadership? What does it mean to be a leader today? And what makes the saints exemplary models of leadership?

These are important questions to tackle if we want to know what kind of leaders we should follow and what kind of leadership characteristics we ourselves want to project in our own lives. The leadership crisis that we are in has been attributed to the fact that we sometimes have the wrong notion of what constitutes an ideal leader. Bill George, in his book *True North*, wrote that "that misguided stand often result in the wrong people attaining critical leadership roles."[24] More often than not, there are individuals aspiring to become leaders ultimately for the prestige, the power, and that elevated status, and wrongfully focusing on, what Bill George identified as the "trappings and spoils of leadership." Perhaps before we select our next leader or before we, ourselves, plunge into a leadership position, we should first take the time to better understand what leadership is, how it is defined, and how we have come to our current understanding of it.

---

[24] Bill George, *True North: Discover Your Authentic Leadership* (San Francisco: Jossey-Bass, 2007).

Leadership: the Word, the Concept, the Trends

One effective way to understand something is to first try to understand the origin of the word. Meanings and interpretations of many of our words in the English language have changed over time. Leadership is one of those words that has gone through many different transformations. We should take a moment to retrace where the word *leadership* comes from and what the word *lead* means, as well as the trends in the development of how we understand the word today.

Lead comes from the old English word *laed*, which means "path" or "road." The verb *laedan* means "to travel." Therefore, a leader is one who goes ahead to show fellow travelers the path.

There seems to be some kind of continuity from this original meaning in how we interpret leadership today. We understand the meaning of leadership today as "to guide." In another ancient context, the word *lead* means "to draw out" as in to draw out information from people. It comes from the Latin word *ductare*, which means to draw out. The Latin noun *ductor* means "a leader." From this Latin root, we get the word *education-adducere*-which means "to draw out."

Thus, when we look at the historical root of the word, *leadership* today has taken on several meanings but are all somehow related. We interpret leadership today as leading others, showing them the way, empowering them, and drawing the best out of them. And, in fact, many who have studied leadership, especially in recent years, will agree that leadership is about inspiring others and drawing out in others their potential to be all that they can be.

The way we interpret leadership now might sound simple, but the word leadership, as well as how we now conceptualize leadership, has gone through many different iterations and interpretations throughout the centuries. The way we view leadership might be different from how leadership was viewed one hundred or one thousand years ago, especially when leadership has evolved dramatically in just the last one hundred years.

The study of leadership has shifted focus several times already, particularly in the last one hundred years, with certain theories fundamentally impacting the way leadership is viewed by people. Leadership scholarship has been transforming constantly. The way we understand and perceive it has been, in so many ways, adaptive to its environment. Many of the leadership views in the past century have been keenly influenced by the changing economic activities and societal developments, particularly from the period of the Industrial Revolution all the way to the beginning of the transition to the knowledge economy. It was during the Industrial Revolution that leadership started to gain recognition as a key component of the economic endeavors of the time. There are different styles of leadership identified by management scholars and social psychologists over this period of transition. One leadership style that dominated the period, from the Industrial Revolution all the way through pretty much the beginning of the knowledge economy of the 1990s, was top-down leadership. Many of us, especially the generations before the millennials, are still accustomed to this top-down leadership—although that sentiment is declining. Many of us have probably experienced working in top-down hierarchical organizations where leadership is authoritative in nature. But if you look around, especially among many of the young start-up companies today, you will get a sense that times have changed and so have the styles of leadership.

In the 1940s, Kurt Lewin, one of the modern pioneers of organizational psychology, theorized that there are three styles of leadership: autocratic, democratic, and laissez-faire.

When things need to get done and you need workers to know how and when things should be done, you need an autocratic leader (also known as authoritarian leader) who can exercise close and top-down control over his or her followers. In this "my way or the highway" style of leadership, the leader makes the decisions, determines the policies, and dictates the tasks but does not have to participate in any of the work. This style of leadership could work when decisions need to be made right away, or it could work in situations where the followers have little to no experience. Nowadays, it is probably the least popular style of leadership, but in reality, in many group situations, it is still one of the most common. Even though it has fallen out of favor in recent decades, remnants of this style of leadership still exists today, and it can probably still be an effective style in certain situations. But as one can imagine, this style, especially when abused, can lead to uncomfortable, dysfunctional, and even hostile environments.

History has a number of infamous autocratic leaders who we can learn from—learn not to absolutely model after. Autocratic leadership is becoming less and less popular because as we get deeper into the knowledge era, this style of leadership is not well-suited for the kinds of social interaction we are now having with one another. We don't like leaders who dictate what we do. And as you can imagine, this style of leadership is also a style that does not suit a leader aspiring for saintliness.

In the kind of society that we now live in, one that is more of a knowledge-based economy, the more popular style of leadership is either the democratic leadership, wherein members are empowered to choose and to collectively make decisions, or the laissez-faire leadership, where the workers are delegated the tasks, the rights, and the power to make decisions. In these situations, the followers are trusted to make the right decisions, and their contributions are valued. Members of the group are valued, respected, and treated with the belief that each member has something important and unique to contribute to the group. We now embrace diversity and place a higher value on it. We recognize that diversity is good for society. Having people from different backgrounds—may it be race, culture, gender, age, personality, thinking style, or skillset— helps to stimulate creativity and insight. And organizations have learned to leverage diversity and the rich ideas generated by the diverse members of their group. In this Age of Information, people are well-informed and are often highly educated. Each individual brings a unique set of skills, values, and characteristics to the group. Good leadership will not only recognize and acknowledge diversity but will capitalize on the varying experiences and unique thoughts that each member brings to the table.

Servant Leader

In the last couple of decades, one of the trends in leadership that has been gaining widespread popularity is servant leadership. *Servant leadership* is a phrase coined by Robert K. Greenleaf in the 1970s. Stephen Covey, the author of the popular book *Seven Habits of Highly Effective People*, believed that servant leadership, as a philosophy and as a practice, will continue to gain relevance in today's modern world. Servant leadership is a leadership style that recognizes and acknowledges the value and the strength of its people. As one can imagine, this is a concept that can be easily adoptable in Christian and religious circles, but to the surprise of many, it is also making strong headway in corporate and business settings. It is taking the principles of leadership up to a whole new level. It is a significant change from the autocratic and authoritarian kind of leadership because now the followers are empowered and elevated almost as if the roles are reversed. In this model, leaders understand their role to be of service to their followers and constituents. It does not mean, however, that the roles of the leader and the followers are totally reversed because that can actually be a misleading conception of the very nature of what servant leadership is. Servant leadership is not about being submissive or docile, allowing the followers to boss the servant-leader around. Servant-leaders leverage the power of their followers by serving them and their needs and by empowering them to become better, healthier, wiser, freer, more autonomous, and more likely themselves to become servant leaders.[25]

Even though the concept of servant leadership as a model is a relatively new trend in leadership studies and practices, it is not a novel and uncommon practice, as evident in the lives of the saints. Our Pope, the highest-ranking leader of the universal Church, has the important title added to his signature: "Servant of the servants of God." Pope Saint Gregory, pope from 590–604, started this tradition, and so, in the last several hundred years, when the serving pope issues a papal bull, one of the Pope's official titles written on that document is "Servant of the servants of God." It is a title that Pope Francis says he is happy to carry out as he goes out serving the servants of God.

We often think of high-profile leaders, such as CEOs, presidents, and generals, not as servants but as leaders who actually have people serving them, like drivers, cooks, and personal assistants. The popes and the saints had a perfect understanding of what servant leadership is and how it works because you can see it in the ways they led their lives. Pope Francis, for instance, recognizes his role as one that is here not to be served but to serve. We have seen him feed the hungry, visit the poor, and tend his flock. He would rather cook his own meals than have someone else serve him his meals. He would even rather ride public transportation. During an interview after his visit to the United States in 2015, he was asked about him becoming a star in the States. He said that the media uses this term "star," but to him, a pope is not a star. He said, "How many stars have we seen go out and fall? On the other hand, being a servant of the servants of God is something that does not pass."[26]

---

[25] Greenleaf, Robert K. *The Servant As Leader* (Cambridge, MA: Center for Applied Studies, 1970).

[26] Linda Bordoni, "Pope Francis: I'm Not a Star, But the Servant of Servants of God." Vatican Radio, September 28, 2015.

This Pope and many of the saints certainly recognized how effective servant leadership is because they lived its core principles and were exceptionally effective at that kind of leadership. They lived and died in service of the people they were leading. They knew servant leadership, its principles, and behaviors, deep in their hearts, because it was ingrained in their prayerful lives by the teachings of Jesus Christ, the ultimate model of servant leadership. It was He who taught us servant leadership two thousand years ago when he said, "The leader among you must become like the one who serves" (Luke 22:26). And it wasn't only what He verbalized; it is what He did. He even washed the feet of His disciples. After He washed their feet, He asked them, "Do you understand what I have done for you?" Through this humble symbolic gesture, He was setting the example for His disciples and for all of us. "For I have set you an example, that you also should do as I have done to you. Very truly, I tell you, servants are not greater than their master, nor are messengers greater than the one who sent them" (John 13:15-16).

The leadership essentials that Jesus Christ taught us over two thousand years ago are the same leadership essentials that the saints have emulated in their own lives. We, in contemporary times, might not recognize that kind of leadership because the Bible only used the term *leader* about a handful of times. *Servant* was the more common term to refer to the leader, but we rarely associate servants and leaders. It just seems paradoxical. However, some of the current leadership trends seem to be heading back to that very fundamental teaching of Christ on servant leadership. After all those years of our scholarly attempts to better understand what exactly leadership is, we have both stretched and narrowed our scope too much and, in the process, lost focus of the true essence of leadership. We did learn a lot about leadership, and we did have a variety of leadership models emerge throughout the last centuries. However, with the recent trends in leadership discussions—especially with the influential voices of the last century's proponents of servant leadership, such as Robert Greenleaf, Peter Senge, and Stephen Covey—our leader-oriented society, through an optimistic set of lenses, seems to be coming back full circle to what Jesus taught us two thousand years ago: to rediscover the real purpose of leadership and its true and timeless essence. Servant-leaders should first and foremost be committed to serving the people.

> *Remember your leaders, who spoke the word of God to you. Consider the outcome of their way of life, and imitate their faith. Jesus Christ is the same yesterday, and today, and forever.*
>
> *—Hebrews 13:7–8*

Leadership Box

There are many different types of leadership, many different styles, and many different leadership traits. Our conceptualization of leadership has evolved over time. Change is constant all around us, and even leadership style is not immune from change. And leadership is different in certain situations. There is leadership in politics; there is leadership in corporations; there is leadership in the church. Leadership studies in the past few decades have been primarily focused on business management models. And there are many great business leaders who can skillfully and successfully lead corporations and teach us about leadership. I can think of several good business leaders. But when you ask someone to think of a leader, it is rare to hear a Catholic saint's name as the first to come to mind. The saints' brand of leadership usually falls outside the leadership box, on the opposite of what society deems as leadership qualities. It is common for us to have preconceived notions of what a leader looks like. We tend to look for someone powerful, someone with authority, someone with a commanding presence, someone outgoing and extroverted, and someone who puts themselves out there. Individuals who have opposite qualities, such as being nice, passive, humble, quiet, or introverted, are easy to miss and dismiss. We tend to skip over those individuals when selecting for leadership positions.

What we need is to not box in ourselves and our thinking of what leadership should be. The saints might not have personalities that match the preconceived leadership qualities that we look for, but they, in fact, make great leaders, especially for today's milieu.

We have commonly portrayed the saints as nice, quiet, introverted people. Some of them might have been, but those were not the prerequisites for sainthood. Actually, some of these saints were stubborn, fiery, and even rowdy. Saint Therese of Lisieux, for example, was a nun who lived a cloistered life, and so one might think that her life was all quiet and introverted; but if you read her autobiography and the accounts of some of the people who knew her, she was a fiery, headstrong, and stubborn young person. And who knew that living a cloistered life, hidden away from the eyes of many, would still qualify her to be one of the most influential and inspirational saints? Saint Therese, who lived such a short life and died at the age of twenty-four, never really was in an earthly position to lead, but now she is leading from heaven, showing us the way, and continues to have a lasting influence on many souls. In 1997, a hundred years after her death, Pope John Paul II declared her Doctor of the Church.

The point is we should be careful not to be misled by any of our tendencies to be biased and try to fit leaders into a box just so that we can label them. Saints come in all shapes and sizes, and they come from all walks of life. Saints can be humble, kind, boisterous, introverted, extroverted, quiet, loud, commanding, obedient, passive, aggressive, contemplative, fiery, stubborn, etc. There is no specific personality trait that could make a person a leader or a saint. What the saints have demonstrated for us, regardless of their personality traits, are some timeless leadership traits that were so effective that they continue to influence and inspire so many lives, even today.

So Old and Yet So New Models of Leadership

The ways we conceptualize leadership have come a long way throughout the centuries, and yet here we are, rediscovering what true leadership is. Jesus Christ demonstrated leadership to us over two thousand years ago when He came down from His kingdom in heaven where He had His seat of power and glory. He came down to earth to humbly take the lowliest place a human can take. Yet we have seen over and over again, throughout the centuries, from early Roman emperors to modern dictators and tyrants, the tendency for leadership to be all about power, authority, dominance, and sometimes total craziness. There is the story of Roman emperor, Caligula, who, whenever he kissed the neck of one of his four wives, would say, "I have the power to have this lovely neck chopped as soon as I say so." Fortunately, the days of such crazy and toxic emperors are over—or at least, less celebrated. However, it does not mean that there are no more half-mad leaders out there garnering a following. Unfortunately, they are still out there.

But just because we haven't had the best models of leadership in the last two thousand years, we must not let that dictate to us what leadership is and should be. We have to keep our standards for leadership elevated. We must not let the leadership that Jesus demonstrated two thousand years ago get overshadowed, forgotten, and brushed off to the side. Jesus showed us leadership that was about humility, servanthood, and partnership. We have had generation after generation of dictators and tyrants who were about ruling over people, accumulating wealth, and gaining glory. We know that these kinds of corrupt and toxic leaders are not what we need in society. What we need is to rediscover the humility and servanthood that the greatest leader, Jesus Christ, demonstrated to us.

Jesus Christ told us this one specific principle of leadership over two thousand years ago: "Anyone who wants to be first must be the very last, and the servant of all" (Mark 9:35).

We seem to have forgotten this. Some of us might remember it and attempt to act it out, but when we do, we come to the realization that it is not easy. It seems counter to the norms dictated by secular society. However, there are signs around today, even in such a secular milieu, that we seem to be recognizing the value of this 2,000-year-old teaching. In the latter part of the last century, many organizations once again started to realize this principle as key to effective leadership. The saints, particularly Saint Francis in the Middle Ages, brought this principle back to societal life, and he did change the Church. He rebuilt the Church. But the kind of leadership he advocated did not make it to the leadership scholars' discussion table until the late 1970s, when Robert Greenleaf coined the phrase "servant leadership." Ever since the coining of that phrase, our perspective on leadership started to shift. It seemed as if our collective conceptualization of leadership would get flipped upside down. In a matter of years, the tides shifted. Society as a whole has gotten much better at not tolerating cruel and erroneous acts of emperors, dictators, and tyrants. We have kicked to curb the days of leaders using people to serve their own personal needs. We know that doesn't work. It does not mean, however, that bad leaders don't exist anymore. They might not be as visible and obvious anymore. Sometimes, they are just good dressing up in sheep's clothing. They might not be throwing chairs around or kicking the tables anymore, but toxic leaders still exist. No matter how good they try to be, we can still detect their inauthenticity. We can still feel them and their negative effects on our organizations. But sometimes, bad leaders may just not realize that they are bad leaders. And some bad leaders become bad by accident or not by their willful intention.

What we need to see a lot of now in leadership is true servant leadership. We need leadership that recognizes that the priority is to serve the needs of the people. We need leadership that values its people. We need leadership that is about humility and selflessness.

Nature or/and Nurture

Do you think that President Lincoln was born to lead? Do you think that Mother Teresa was born to lead? What about you? Do you think that you were born to lead? Do you think that you would make a good leader?

This is another important debate in the leadership discussions. We seem to have an insatiable desire to know whether leaders are born or made. Just like the other virtues, skills, and attributes, the social sciences have subjected leadership to the nature versus nurture debate as well. But just like what we know about the other nature/nurture debates, it is perhaps fair to say that leadership is not just something that is by DNA design gifted to only a select few at birth. Although, in a 2013 University College of London study,[27] researchers found a specific leadership gene sequence that is associated with the tendency for individuals to occupy a leadership position. Such a study suggests that leadership is partly hereditary and some leaders have these distinctive dispositional characteristics when they are born.

Nonetheless, there is strong evidence and a general consensus

---

[27] Jan-Emmanuel De Neve, Slava Mikhaylov, Christopher T. Dawes, Nicholas A. Christakis, James H. Fowler. "Born to lead? A twin design and genetic association study of leadership role occupancy." *The Leadership Quarterly*, 2013; 24 (1)

that leadership is still predominantly a skill that can be acquired, learned, and developed. The same researchers of that University College of London study were quick to point out that effort is still a vital aspect of leadership development. We may not be born with the identified genes for leadership, but we are still capable of becoming leaders. It is our calling, after all, and we just have to work at it and pursue it. In the Philippines where I grew up, there is a popular saying:

"*Nasa Diyos ang awa; nasa tao ang gawa.*" Translated into English, it means, "Mercy resides in God; deeds are in men." If we want it, we have to work at it. God reward us for our hard work.

Pursuing leadership is like bike-riding. Many of us have the ability to learn how to ride a bike, and many of us can bike, but not all of us are meant to be elite cycling champions. I suppose that we can if we really wanted to but not all of us will equally pursue that possibility. I love cycling and I have been cycling for years. I would love to be an elite cyclist but I know that I have predispositions in life that limit me from becoming one. Those who want to become bike champions know that they would have to spend years and years training. Champion riders know that getting to the top takes a lot of effort. But it doesn't mean that I should give up the work to becoming a good cyclist. I still can be a good cyclist.

Leaders are born, and all human beings born are called to lead. Leadership is, as Stephen Covey said, our birthright, and our ability to lead is not a fixed trait that we are born with nor does it develop fully overnight. Leadership ability has to be nurtured. Just like with any other talent or ability we have, we must still put in the effort to nurture it to make it useful. We need to have a growth mindset versus having a fixed mindset when thinking about leadership. Every single day on earth is an opportunity to grow, improve, and maximize our God-given potential.

We have to scratch the thinking that we can never be leaders or that we just don't have the qualities to be leaders. We may never be leaders on the world stage or even the top of a corporate ladder,

Lessons in Leadership from the Saints

but we, in our own personal ways and in our own personal sphere, can improve our leadership abilities and be leaders to the people around us, the people we love, the people we are responsible for.

Looking at the saints' lives and stories, they nurtured their leadership abilities similar to the way they nurtured their saintliness. They were nurtured by the people around them, their families, and the people that surrounded them, and most important, they were nurtured by constant prayer and the constant discernment of the will of God. Their saintly deeds and leadership acts did not just happen one day. It was not just one great act of sainthood or martyrdom that defined their saintly lives. In fact, their entire lives were spent training and growing so that they could prepare for the moments when God called them to be leaders and to be holy. The saints have what is called a "growth mindset." They did not yield to the thinking that saintliness or leadership is just for the select gifted few. They knew that holiness or leadership qualities were not fixed traits. They understood that there is plenty of room for growth and improvement in the Christian journey. They heard God's calling, stood up, and responded to the call. They pursued holiness with vigor and continued to do God's will until they drew their last breath.

Stewart Friedman, author of the book *Total Leadership* and *Leading the Life You Want*,[28] where he profiled some notable figures like Michelle Obama and Bruce Springsteen, concluded that people are not born to be great leaders. Friedman says that becoming a great leader requires persistence, passion, discipline, and courage to pursue what is important to you and to the people around you. Leadership is a skill—a learned or acquired ability and not a quality that people are born with. It is a skill available to us. It is a calling to us all, but we have to go after it. Some say that leadership can be taught, but we neglect the step of choosing

---

[28] Stewart Friedman. *Total Leadership: Be a Better Leader, Have a Richer Life* (Boston, MA: Harvard Business Review Press, 2014).

the path that forms us. Learning leadership is a two-way street. Someone can spend the time and effort teaching leadership, but we, the recipients, must spend the time and effort pursuing it, learning it, and wanting it. Leaders are born. Leaders are made. These statements don't have to be contradictory. Leaders are born in the sense that we all are born on this earth. Leaders are made in the sense that we all have the calling to lead. We need to recognize that leadership is a skill that can be taught, practiced, and sharpened. And it takes an entire lifetime to develop. Leadership is always a work in progress. Leadership can always be improved.

A Lifetime Spent Nurturing, Training, Practicing, and Praying

Leadership, along with saintliness, is an attribute that takes a lifetime to develop. Both need to be practiced, honed, and sharpened.

I am reminded of the story of Saint Maximilian Kolbe. For a long time, the only thing I knew about Saint Maximilian Kolbe was the event where he offered his life in order to save the life of a fellow prisoner in Auschwitz prison camp during World War II. So that entire time, not knowing anything else about the rest of his life, Saint Maximilian Kolbe's legacy to me was defined by that one heroic deed. That alone was definitely heroic and noteworthy, but that is not the only thing he did to become a saint. Unfortunately for me, that was all I knew about Saint Maximilian Kolbe until I started to delve deeper into his life. And the more I learned about Saint Maximilian Kolbe, the more I realized that there was actually more to his life story—a whole lot of other noteworthy deeds. I began to discover that that one instance, that one heroic moment in the Nazi concentration camp where he gave up his life for another man, is actually a culmination of all the decades he spent praying, serving God, practicing very holy deeds, and growing in holiness. Everything he had done leading up to that moment of martyrdom was, in so many ways, training and preparing him for that one great moment. His preparation for leadership, for saintliness, and eventual martyrdom for the faith, started at a very young age. Since childhood, he had been praying fervently to God and to the Blessed Virgin Mary. One day while praying and discerning God's will for him, he had a vision of the Virgin Mary. He would recount that incident later as an adult:

> "That night I asked the Mother of God what was to become of me. Then she came to me holding two crowns, one white, the other red. The white one meant that I should persevere in purity, and the red that I should become a martyr. She asked me if I was willing to accept either of these crowns. I said that I would accept them both."

When he got older, he left his home to pursue God's calling and joined the Franciscan religious order. He became a priest and later a missionary, preaching the gospel and performing God's work in Europe and in Asia.

He founded a monastery in Japan, which continues to be prominent in Japanese Catholicism today. There is actually a fascinating story about this monastery. When Saint Maximilian was in the early stages of building the monastery, many people criticized how and where that monastery was built. The critics thought that it was foolishly built at the worst possible location and that it was not in harmony with nature. But Saint Maximilian accepted the criticisms with kindness and pushed on to finish construction by 1931. It became a home for the Franciscans in Japan. It was called the Garden City of the Immaculata. Fourteen years later during World War II, when the atomic bomb was dropped on Nagasaki, the entire city was flattened except for the monastery—the monastery that Saint Maximilian Kolbe built despite critics believing it to be in the worst possible location.

Saint Maximilian Kolbe spent his entire life dedicated to God's work. Despite deteriorating health due to tuberculosis, he served God all the way to the end. He built the monastery, he served in foreign missions, and he established and operated a religious publishing press. He tirelessly advanced the work of promoting devotion to the Immaculate Mary. Even in Auschwitz, he was teaching and ministering to his fellow prisoners about the love of God.

He had been spending his entire life in preparation for that one ultimate gesture of love. In Auschwitz, whenever one prisoner appeared to have escaped, the Nazi commandant, in reprisal, would order ten other prisoners from the camp to die by starvation. Well, one day, there was such an incident. One prisoner, Franciszek Gajowniczek, was then randomly selected and called out of formation, but as he stepped forward, he begged and cried out, "My wife! My children!"

When Maximilian Kolbe heard this, he was moved with compassion even though he did not know the man. He broke ranks, stepped forward, and said to the guard, "I will take that man's place." The guard asked who he was, and he replied with basically the last words we hear from him, "I am a Catholic priest." Not only did he choose to offer his life in place of this man, but he was also choosing to be a martyr for his Catholic faith. The switch between Maximilian and Franciszek was permitted. Saint Maximilian Kolbe was sent to die.

That one moment of martyrdom, that one ultimate sacrifice, was the conclusion that wrapped up all the things he had done his entire life—the prayer, his devotion to the Blessed Virgin Mary, his service, and his continuous and tireless works of selflessness. He had been sharpening his craft of love—love for his fellow men and for God. His growth and maturity through prayer and constant conversation with God led him to that one ultimate act of love. And so when that moment arrived, he knew right away what he had to do.

> *Let us remember that love lives through sacrifice and is nourished by giving. Without sacrifice there is no love.*
>
> *—Maximilian Kolbe*

Unless a grain of wheat falls into the ground and dies, it dies alone; but if it dies, it bears much fruit (see John 12:24). Saint Maximilian Kolbe died for one man, but his works and his mission continues and flourishes. Franciszek Gajowniczek, whose life was saved by Saint Maximilian Kolbe, was liberated from the concentration camp and lived another fifty years. He spent the rest of his life-giving talks about the heroic act of love of Maximilian Kolbe. The church today gets the benefit of knowing about Saint Maximilian Kolbe because of this man. Thousands of followers are inspired by what he had done not only to spare this one man's life, but by the countless other acts of love and charity he had done his entire life. One of the prolific early Christian writers, Tertullian, said, "The blood of the martyrs is the seed of the church." Today, the Militia of Immaculata, the Catholic evangelization movement that Saint Maximilian Kolbe founded about one hundred years ago, has grown and spread internationally with over three million members. Saint Maximilian has indeed planted that seed for the church, giving spiritual renewal and consecrating Catholics to the Blessed Virgin Mary.

And that is what leadership is about. Leadership is not just a one-time incident, and it does not happen overnight. That life story of Maximilian Kolbe shows us that leadership, as well as saintliness, develops and continues to develop over an entire lifetime, until the very end. Some leaders might have that one shining moment, and they might end up being recognized for it. The truth is, we have to spend the time getting ready for that one moment by refining and sharpening our leadership abilities daily. Pope Francis did not become a leader overnight. He started early in his life when he committed to the call to the religious life. And so, even as a priest and leader of his parish, he continually spent time developing, refining, and sharpening his leadership. We won't all be popes or bishops, but we have the potential to be able to lead. It is our calling to draw out this potential to lead, but we have to continuously nurture that potential by constantly praying and discerning God's will. We have to seek His guidance and His wisdom so that when the moment comes for us to step up and lead, we will be ready to step forward and be able to carry out the task and the will of God.

For Ardent Love –
Saint Maximilian Kolbe, faithful follower of Saint Francis of Assisi, inflamed by the love of God you dedicated your life to the practice of virtue and to works of the apostolate. Look down with favor upon us who devoutly confide in your intercession. Having consecrated yourself to the Immaculate Virgin Mary, you inspired countless souls to a holy life and to various forms of the apostolate in order to do good to others and to spread the kingdom of God. Obtain for us the grace by our lives and labors to draw many souls to Christ. In your close conformity to our Divine Savior, you reached such an intense degree of love that you offered your life to save a fellow prisoner. Implore God that we, inflamed by such ardent charity, may through our living faith and our apostolic works witness Christ to our fellow man, and thus merit to join you in the blessed vision of God.
Amen.

Spiritual Intelligence

Leadership and spirituality are two entities that are rarely discussed together. However, in many recent leadership studies, spiritual intelligence (SQ) among leaders is making strong headway. Many of us have heard of the importance of IQ (intelligence quotient) and EQ (emotional intelligence) but SQ, not so much. We are familiar with the notion of how important it is for someone in a leadership role to have a certain level of intelligence. We want our leaders to be smart, witty, learned, educated, etc. Although sometimes we do have the tendency to limit the concept of intelligence and to think of it simply as cognitive intelligence. Intelligence is a lot more than just the ability to use one's brain. We tend to put a heavy emphasis on this kind of intelligence, and general mental ability is undoubtedly an important predictor of leadership effectiveness. However, that is not all that matters, and it is probably not even the most important when it comes to what we expect from our leaders. The brain does matter, but it's not the only thing that matters. Cognitive intelligence is just one narrow aspect of leadership. Leading people is not all about being intellectually or technically smart, but it is also about how we go about interacting with the people around us. Leadership is also about emotional intelligence (EQ).

Research findings by Daniel Goleman, author of the book that gave the term "emotional intelligence" widespread popularity in the 1990s, suggest that the most effective leaders have a high degree of emotional intelligence. Leaders with a high level of EQ are able to use emotional information to lead the people around them and to facilitate problem-solving and goal-attainment. They are aware of their own emotions as well as others' emotions. In today's complex society, where there is a rich diversity and a variety of viewpoints, we have to exercise our emotional intelligence to maintain healthy relationships with one another. There is no doubt that EQ is an essential skill for leaders to have in order to be able to lead and develop others, especially in this diverse and complex society we live in. Having EQ competence means being able to knit together the diversity into working constructively and harmoniously with one another.

Having high EQ is a lot more than just being nice and being able to play with others in the sandbox. It is about being able to manage the diversity and even the conflicting agendas with adherence to the standards, the morals, and the vision. Mother Teresa was a strong and tough leader, and there were many times she needed to be. She had a job to do, and there were people who did not always give her support or agree with her. She had the ability to converse with all people, from global leaders, politicians, and journalists, to the poorest beggars. She had a way to communicate to others about her vision, her mission, and God's love. She communicated sincerely, with care and with a smile. Mother Teresa would often say, "Peace begins with a smile."

> *Where most men work for degrees after their names, we work for one before our names: "Saint."*
>
> *—Mother Angelica*

To even take a step further and take leadership beyond cognitive intelligence and emotional intelligence, there is what's currently making its rounds in the leadership discussion, spiritual intelligence or SQ. SQ is a relatively new and emerging concept in the field of psychology and/or philosophy, but it is an important dimension, a higher dimension as some might say, that must be factored in when it comes to understanding leadership. In fact, Stephen Covey argued that it is the most central and most fundamental of all the intelligences because it serves as a source of guidance for all the other intelligences. SQ is the type of intelligence that allows us to recognize that inner voice of our noble and higher self.

IQ, EQ, and SQ Embodied

The SQ dimension of leadership, when integrated with IQ and EQ, together can take leadership up to a whole new level. SQ leadership takes its incumbents to a higher stage of human development.

Danah Zohar, the author who coined the term "spiritual intelligence" and one of the leading authors on SQ, identified twelve principles underlying SQ:[29]

1. Self-awareness
2. Vision and value-led
3. Positive use of adversity
4. Holistic
5. Compassion
6. Celebration of diversity
7. Field-independent
8. Ask fundamental "why" questions
9. Ability to reframe the situations
10. Spontaneity
11. Sense of vocation
12. Humility

It is relatively easy to call to mind someone who is a leader with a high IQ or a high EQ, or maybe even a leader with a high IQ and a high EQ all at the same time in one package. But try to think of leaders with a high IQ, a high EQ, and a high SQ all in one. The SQ is a different level of maturity, even for those who are already good, smart leaders. It takes a lifetime of pruning, refining, and praying to find leaders who embody the twelve principles of SQ.

This list of characteristics seems high ideals but finding

---

[29] Zohar, D., *SQ: Connecting with Our Spiritual Intelligence* (London: Bloomsbury, 2000).

leadership that embodies all three types of intelligence is not impossible. I can think of individuals who have modeled these traits for us. Looking at the twelve principles of SQ, there is a pool of such leaders among the saints who have gone through some of the most intense tests and trials and have emerged to be high in SQ, IQ, and EQ. I can name a few saints who exhibit these leadership qualities. Think about the exemplary deeds of Mother Teresa, Saint Ignatius, Saint Francis Xavier, Saint Dominic, Saint John Bosco—just to name a few. They were humble, vision-led, value-led, compassionate, positive, and had a great sense of their vocation. They had a high degree of IQ and EQ competence that enabled them to do the great things that they did. They built schools; they ran orphanages, and they found a way to accomplish what they set out to do. But on top of their IQ and EQ competencies, what makes them stand out even more as great leaders and great saints is that they had the *spiritual intelligence*. They were always able to see the deeper meaning of life and the bigger picture.

Think about the field-independent Saint Francis Xavier, who was out, often alone, in the field doing God's work. He was in a faraway land, far from his other Jesuit peers and from his leader and mentor, Saint Ignatius; but he came through and persevered. Saint Francis Xavier and the other saints made positive use of adversity. Their encounter with adversity made them stronger because they turned to God for strength and courage.

They were able to reframe the situations and resolve the issues. They were wise and discerning, always consulting and conversing with God, always seeking His wisdom. They started their mission and their days in conversation with God, in prayer, making sure that the work they were doing aligned with the will of God.

They had a good understanding of the ultimate goal of human existence. As servants of others, they understood our role as children of God and that we are all destined to know God's love. Therefore, they cared for others. They illuminated the path for their brothers and sisters in Christ, and they led us. They were leaders who worked well with others because they were humble and genuinely selfless. In their humility, they understood that they were servants of God and that they were servants to the servants of God.

> *If we really want to have eternal life, let us learn all there is to know about eternal Wisdom. If we wish to have roots of immortality deeply embedded in our heart, we must have in our mind knowledge of eternal Wisdom. To know Jesus Christ incarnate Wisdom, is to know all we need.*
>
> *—Saint Louis De Montfort*

TIMES ARE CHANGING

In times like today, the need to have effective, ethical, moral, and just overall good leadership is even more pressing. We need to have the right models of leadership—leadership that we can trust, that we can have faith in, that we can rightfully follow and imitate.

Being a leader as well as being holy these days are both incredibly challenging tasks. Many of the saints that we are modeling after lived in the distant past. The cultural forces of today are significantly different—not necessarily more challenging or less challenging—just different. The surrounding cultural forces change over time and so do the challenges and opportunities. As aspiring leaders and saints, we do need to acknowledge the challenges and the circumstances of the times we are living in. We do need to recognize that the times have changed and are constantly changing.

With societal culture and psychological and spiritual developments so intertwined, spiritual development today is probably not going to be the same as the spiritual development that the saints experienced in the past. Even with the major established religions themselves, despite centuries of long-standing and deeply ingrained traditions, the transmission of practices, beliefs, and teachings from one generation to the next is becoming more difficult. And when the religious traditions do get transmitted to the next generation, they are rarely unaltered.

You might agree with some observers who have concluded

that the influence of religion is declining, particularly if you live in the western part of the globe. Many of you might feel that we live in a society that is much less religious than previous generations. You are not alone in that thinking. Our society's move toward secularism might sound like it is just anecdotal information, but there is some data that can serve as evidence to that. There is the secularization thesis, which is probably the most hotly debated topic in the sociology of religion since the beginning of the latter half of the twentieth century, that suggests that religion declines as society progresses through modernization.

Pew Research, a think tank that conducts scientific survey studies of various social issues on a regular basis, found in their recent survey that the importance of religion and the religious affiliations of Americans have been on a steady decline ever since as recent as 2007. The fastest growing cohort, which is now 23 percent of the American population compared to 16 percent in 2007, are Americans who prefer to have no religious affiliation.[30]

In a separate study that looked at the General Social Survey (GSS) data,[31] the percentage of adults in the United States who have no religious preference more than doubled since the 1970s, with a sharp increase in the 1990s, and has been steadily rising since. In 2014, 21 percent of the American population preferred no religion. So if you feel as if we, as a society, are becoming less religious and less spiritual, consider these studies and you might find your observation and your feelings to be valid.

With the changing times, we, in our modern lives, are becoming less and less dependent on God, and the world we live in now is remarkably distinct from the generations past. Mobile phones, the Internet, personal computers, tablets, Facebook, and Twitter are things that are widespread and deeply ingrained in

---

[30] Pew Research Center. *2014 Religious Landscape Study.*
[31] Michael Hout & Tom W. Smith, "Fewer Americans Affiliate with Organized Religion, Belief and Practice Unchanged: Key Findings from the 2014 General Social Survey." (March 10, 2015).

our culture now, but these are things that did not exist just a few years ago. Many of those things were not around in previous generations. I was a young kid not too long ago, and I remember playing with non-digital and non-electronic things. I played with twigs, sticks, and rocks. Now, kids these days are inseparable from their tablets and digital screens. Some of these things that are now a prominent and apparently a necessary part of our society did not even exist at all a generation ago. I certainly did not have a cell phone or a social media account as a teenager, but now I find it hard to imagine daily life without those things. I used to get around just fine without a GPS but now I can't imagine driving to a new location without a GPS. Many of these things only started existing in the last several years, but look at how much they have changed our lives and our society within such a short time span. Having been around for over forty years now, I have witnessed first-hand many societal changes. The speed of change in the last several years is amazing. Some are drastic changes, some are gradual. Nonetheless, society today is remarkably different from the 1970s, for sure. Imagine how much more remarkable the difference is between today and hundreds of years ago. Imagine how different our world today is compared to Saint Francis's thirteenth-century world or Saint Augustine's fifth-century world.

Not only have the changes over the years been so dramatic but the pace of life is so much faster. There used to be a time when making dinner was a three-hour process. Preparing dinner used to be so meticulously labor intense. But now, one can have dinner in a matter of minutes, even seconds. Back in the day, there was no such thing as drive-through fast food. Now we are quick to complain if we do not get our happy meal in under ninety seconds at the fast-food drive-through.

Sometimes, news companies, who are supposed to be the poster child for speed, are even late in getting to some breaking news because someone from a remote place in China has already tweeted about an earthquake that just happened seconds ago.

Snail mail used to not be snail-paced at all because it was really faster than the pony express. But now snail mail has become such. Our playful use of the word *viral* now means something completely different, especially when compared to the much more serious use of the word *viral* during the Dark Ages and the years of the plague.

Before modern cars, traveling to the next town used to take days, even weeks. Nowadays, we are used to getting to places and obtaining things we need and want right away.

The call to holiness is perennially the same but the environment that the called are in is not. Imagine how these changes are impacting our response, our psyche, our societal and spiritual life, and even our virtues.

Patience: The Lost Virtue

In the past, the delay of gratification was probably a much easier exercise as it was often necessary. Some of the hardships we can only imagine today were just a usual part of someone's normal daily life in the old days. I remember hearing stories from my parents and grandparents that they used to walk for miles in slippers just to get to school. I recognize some of the locations they would talk about, and I know that I can only get to those places now in something with wheels; otherwise, it would take hours to get to them.

With fast food, with one-hour delivery, with a lot of our material needs instantly available at our fingertips, in our society of instant gratification, there are some basic human skills and attitudes that get lost or underused and underdeveloped. Pope John Paul II used to warn us against becoming the "civilization of consumerism" and "slaves of possession and of immediate gratification."[32] These are the signs of the times. Thanks to humanity's ingenuity and our technological innovations, a lot of our daily routines are much more convenient and comfortable. However, in the process of making our lives easier and more comfortable, we have made the cultural forces that condition some of our muscles, particularly our patience muscles, a little laxer. Our patience muscles do not get as developed as they used to in the older days. The spiritual gymnasium that we now have in the world is different compared to that of our predecessors', and our spiritual character just doesn't get that conditioning that our predecessors got. Without our patience muscles and other spiritual muscles beefed up, it becomes extra challenging to emulate the lives of the saints who have come before us.

> *Patience is the companion of wisdom.*
>
> *—Saint Augustine*

In 1970, Walter Mischel and his colleagues at Stanford University conducted the study that has become one of the most well-known experiments in the behavioral studies—the Marshmallow Experiment. The experiment was designed to see what strategies preschool-aged children take to resist the temptation of eating a marshmallow set right in front of them by researchers who then left the room. The children were instructed not to eat the marshmallows for at least fifteen minutes until the researcher came back in the room. They were told that if they were able to resist the urge, they would get rewarded with a second marshmallow. Some of the children were able to resist and hold out for the second marshmallow; some were not.

---

[32] Pope John Paul II, *Sollicitudo Rei Socialis,* Encyclical to the Bishops, Priests, Religious Families, sons and daughters of the Church and all people of good will for the 20th anniversary of Populorum Progressio.

Fast forward several years; the same children were studied as a follow-up to this experiment. What they found was that the children in the Marshmallow Study who were able to hold out longer as young kids showed better life outcomes in their young adult lives, including having higher SAT scores, better educational attainment, and even better BMI (body mass index).

Since this groundbreaking study, the ability to delay gratification, not just as children but as adults, has been linked, either scientifically or anecdotally, to marriages and divorces, sexuality, addictive behaviors, spending habits, career choices, the pursuit of higher education, and even sanctity. To be able to delay immediate gratification for a more positive future consequence is indeed an ability that pays. Patience is indeed a virtue that leads to positive outcomes.

So now in our world with microwaves, fast food, lightning-speed e-mail, texting, and other tools and technologies that have dramatically sped up our lives, one is led to wonder where we stand on our ability to be patient and delay gratification. With our modern advances in society today, particularly in our technologies and our societal values, the ability to delay our gratification seems like it might be a lost skill. Patience is an ability that is now getting undermined.

Can we still patiently wait three hours for dinner to be ready? Are we still able to wait a couple of days for information to travel via snail mail? A text just came in, but can we still manage to wait a little longer to pick up our smartphone? Do we absolutely have to read that text right now while we are driving? There seems to be a correlation between decreasing patience and increasing texting-and-driving accidents. If you get a craving right now, you do not have to wait too long anymore because there is fast food. If we have any material need, it might feel like it is our entitlement that we ought to be able to meet that need immediately. We have certain expectations to meet our material needs and even wants. Thanks to technological progress of the last century or so, we have set up our environments to allow for our material needs and wants to be met right away. It is not necessarily a negative thing. Progress is good, and I don't think a lot of us have an inclination to want to go back in time and live in the days before cell phones or digital technology. I've already thrown away my Rolodex and my printed driving maps. I don't think there is anything wrong with advancing in our progress as a human race, and we can always strive for progress and improving our lives. But as we continue making progress and making our human lives better, we must not lose sight of the things that are important.

> *For this very reason, make every effort to add to your faith, goodness; and to goodness, knowledge; and to knowledge, self-control; and to self-control, perseverance; and to perseverance, godliness; and to godliness, mutual affection; and to mutual affection, love. For if you possess these qualities in increasing measure, they will keep you from being ineffective and unproductive in your knowledge of our Lord Jesus Christ.*
>
> *—2 Peter 1:5–8*

Holy Patience

Dietrich von Hildebrand, a Catholic philosopher and theologian, wrote about "Holy Patience" and the patient man[33] and said that: "The requirements of the moment, no matter how imperious, can never displace or overshadow his attention to higher values." Patience is a virtue. It allows us to be humble and

---

[33] Dietrich von Hildebrand, *Transformation in Christ: On the Christian Attitude* (San Francisco, CA: Ignatius Press, 1990).

to submit to God's perfect will. It is the ultimate act of surrender to God. God has His timing, and we must not be too focused on ourselves that we forget God's sovereignty over time. We must not forget that it is God who "determines the proper day and hour for the fruitful performance of certain actions and even more exclusively, the ripening of our seeds and the harvest of our labors."[34]

A Merry Christmas?

We have to recognize that with the kind of society we live in, our patience muscles are underused and underdeveloped, and we need to be aware of the challenges that this brings to our spiritual warfare and to our leadership development. Let's face it: we live in a societal system that encourages materialism, overconsumption, and instant gratification. Just look at the subtle changes to how we celebrate Christmas. Having celebrated Christmas over forty times now in my lifetime and also in different cultural settings, I can't help but notice the changes over time in how we celebrate and perceive the Christmas holidays. Several weeks, maybe even months, before Christmas, advertisements will start dominating our TV screens, newspapers, radio, and computers, incessantly bombarding us with messages about what new toys and gadgets we should get for the holidays. Maybe it's just me, but as I look back, I don't recall having seen this many toys and gadgets advertised growing up as a child. It is a relatively modern tradition that is having a curious impact on us Christians and the way we think about Christmas.

Psychology researchers Tim Kasser and Kennon Sheldon, in their 2002 study published in the *Journal of Happiness*, found

---

[34] Hildebrand, *Transformation in Christ: On the Christian Attitude*, p.328.

that during the Christmas season, the more people focus on materialistic aims, such as spending money on gifts and receiving gifts from others, the less focus they have on spiritual aims and the true meaning of Christmas. The more they focus on material things, the less merrier their Christmas season is. The participants of their study reported more happiness when family and religious experiences were more predominant during the Christmas season; the participants reported less happiness when the more materialistic elements of Christmas were more predominant.[35] Material gifts during Christmas, as many Christians probably have suspected, do not necessarily make people happy.

The commercialization and the evolution of Christmas traditions over the years is just an example of how the conditions around us, the distractions and diversions, make our imitation of Christ much more challenging. Even in the good old days of the sixteenth century, Saint Teresa of Avila noted: "We tend to get lost in our worldly affairs: buying and selling, grasping and indulging, falling into spiritual error and rising up again." That challenge has not gone away but has, in so many ways, become more challenging. Thinking about Black Friday sales or what new, fancy toy to buy just makes it so much easier for us to lose sight of what the Christmas season is truly about. The prevalence and the magnitude of these recent commercialized additions to the Christmas tradition have clouded our perception of the holidays with materialistic aspirations. With all these diversions and distractions, we forget that Christmas is about giving—not of worldly, materialistic things, but of love and life. The most important gift we receive during Christmas, just as the tradition itself is supposed to be celebrating, is the gift from God, the gift of His Son. The most important gift we can give others is the gift of ourselves. As Pope John Paul II used to say, we must not focus on

---

[35] Kasser, T. & Sheldon, K.M. "What Makes for a Merry Christmas," *Journal of Happiness*, 3 (2002), 313–329.

having; we should be focused on *being*. It is definitely challenging, but we need to shift our focus from having or obtaining things to *being*—being a father or a mother, being a friend, being a Christian.

The Good Old Days

Spiritual warfare these days is not the same as the spiritual warfare in the past. We need to recognize what the saints went through in their unique life circumstances and what we are now up against in our own times. Philosophers and theologians continuously grapple with the meaning of God, religion, and spirituality in our present age. We live in a world that is becoming increasingly more and more complex, more technological, more diverse, more digital, more globalized, more interconnected, more fast-paced, busier, and so on and so forth. The changes we experience as a society are becoming increasingly more rapid and more dramatic. Unless you have been living under a rock for the last twenty years, our world has witnessed one major technological innovation after another, all within just a few blinks of the eye. We went from beepers to smartphones just like that. These are changes that have a profound impact on our attitudes, thinking, and worldviews. And that makes our current society unique and different from the previous generations.

For example, consider the dramatic changes that each generation has gone through. Consider the stark differences among the generations around today. Each one of them is shaped by circumstances unique to their generation. The Vietnam War, the counterculture movement, and other significant events were some of the factors that shaped the worldviews of the older generations. And then, within a lifespan, cell phones, the Internet, and other technological changes entered the scene. These are some of the major factors that are now dramatically and drastically shaping the worldviews of the younger generations. And these are generations that barely even span one hundred years, yet the life experiences of each generation are remarkably different from one another.

And so, as we consider how the saints can serve as our models of leadership and holiness, you might be wondering how we can possibly relate to them when they lived so many years ago. The circumstances we are in now are just so different from theirs. We often find it difficult to relate to someone different from us. In terms of generational differences, we can find it difficult to relate to our grandparents or to our grandchildren. Our differences there can only span a few years or decades. So how exactly do we try to relate to someone who lived centuries ago? Many of the saints we highlight in this book were from times that are so vastly different than ours: Saint Augustine from the fifth century, Saint Francis of Assisi from the thirteenth century, Saint Ignatius from the sixteenth century. Even one of the most recent saints, Padre Pio, for example, lived not too long ago, and yet the differences compared to the time we now live in—with all this technology, where everything we own is digital and electronic and connected to the web—seem so distant.

Padre Pio, for example, lived less than a hundred years ago, and yet how many of us today can say that we have the same childhood experience as his? He lived from 1887 to 1968 in a small Italian province and grew up in a household that did not have much at all in terms of material possessions. He grew up in a large family that prayed the rosary daily and went to Mass every Sunday. He grew up tending sheep and taking care of the family land and the animals. His father, despite not knowing how to read or write, knew all the stories of the Bible by heart, and he would share those stories with the young Padre Pio. You can just imagine how much this focus on God, starting from early childhood, would influence Padre Pio's spiritual development and vocation choices. But in your social network, how many do you know grew up in that kind of environment, tending land and sheep, praying the rosary daily, with not many possessions, and who can recite verses of the Bible? The environment that Padre Pio grew up in is an environment and a lifestyle so far removed from many of our twenty-first-century lives.

Growing up in such an environment certainly had an impact on Padre Pio's decision to pursue the religious life and holiness. Society, the cultural environment, and our upbringing can have a major role in our own personal development and the choices we make in our lives. We recognize that the times we are living in are different from the days of past. We live in a remarkably complicated environment, but it is not to say that the saints of previous generations did not live in their own complicated environments. Their times were complicated in their own unique ways, and they certainly had their own issues and challenges. They had wars, famines, deadly diseases, and other adversities. One of the things that makes our time unprecedentedly complicated is the kinds of diversions that we now have. Cell phones, tablets, wearable electronics, social media, digital everything, etc., are all new and unprecedented in human history, and these are the hallmarks of the times we live in. I used to sport a beeper growing up, and that was the cool thing to have on your belt back in those days. And even that was not too long ago. By today's technology standards, beepers are unheard of already. The millennials I talk to consider that super old technology and they're practically obsolete. So just imagine the times that the saints lived in. They feel so long ago and so remote, leaving us to wonder just how exactly we can use their examples in today's contemporary scenarios.

I grew up in the 1980s, when video games were just starting to become a prevalent part of a child's life, so I know firsthand how much time it takes away from meditating, praying, or contemplating personal eternal salvation. According to a 2015 survey, our young people today spend, on average, nine hours per day on entertainment media, and that does not even include the use of media on homework or schoolwork.[36] Those are nine precious hours taken away from other important things in life, such as social interactions or prayer or reflection. Some of the largest and oldest religious orders, especially the most well-known ones—the Franciscans, the Dominicans, and the Jesuits—were all founded in the Middle Ages, way before the digital age. The most recent saints canonized were born in the early 1900s. One of these saints, Pope Saint John Paul II, the church leader that I had growing up, was born in 1920 and died in 2005. So how can we post-modern generations, living in the comfort of the Information Age relate to some of these saints? The times we live in are different. Our attitudes, behaviors, virtues, and spirituality can be easily shaped and molded by our social environment, which, in so many ways, is remarkably different from generations past. It's not a criticism of modernity and all the diversions it brings, but it's really a question of what it means to be a Christian today. What does it mean to be a follower of Christ who lived two thousand years ago? And what can the saints who followed Christ in their own times, with their own different challenges, teach us? What can the saints who lived so long ago teach us, and how can we apply those teachings to our modern lives? The call to holiness has not changed over time but the social setting has dramatically changed.

The ways we interact with one another today are different and, in so many ways, unprecedented. In the workplace, where much of the generational research is focused, all five generations—the traditionalists, the baby boomers, Gen X, Gen Y, Gen2020—are now working side by side for the first time in history. People are living longer, and times are changing dramatically. The generations are marked by the cultural forces influencing them and binding them together. On a global scale, generations, as well

---

[36] Common Sense Media. *Common Sense Census: Media Use by Tweens and Teens* (Nov. 3, 2015).

as world cultures, are intermingling. The forces of globalization are keeping us interconnected and making our world smaller and smaller. Many of these situations and circumstances we are in today are new to humanity. The leadership demands dictated by the times are different than in years past.

And so, again, in the midst of these complexities, diversities, and challenges, the questions we have to tackle are:

How do we meet those leadership demands?

How do we find and mold leaders who can step up to today's unique challenges?

If we look to the saints as our models for leadership, how can we relate to them and how can their models apply to our challenges today?

Different Currents, Same Destination

Despite the different kinds of obstacles that we face in today's society, there is no doubt that there will still be saints who will continue to emerge in our lifetime and in the future. The worst of situations often brings the best out of people. Some of the worst times are the times when the ordinary becomes extraordinary. No matter what time or era, there is something about the call of God to His people that just transcends time, culture, and situation. As G. K. Chesterton observed, it is a paradox that each generation is converted by the saint who contradicts it most. No matter what time and place, God will call. And there is something phenomenal and indescribable about how God's people who hear and heed that call respond with all their hearts and minds. There is something about their response, their deeds, their actions, and their faith that profoundly reflect the core essence of what it means to be human, to be God's children, even when it means going against the grain of the current societal norms. Sure, the times are different compared to the days of old. The challenges the generations face today are, in many ways, new waters and are unprecedented in history. Yet, God's call is the same. Every body of water has its own currents, but it is still the destination that dictates the direction where the boat is headed. Our desire to reach our destination drives us, and it does not matter what direction the currents are going. Regardless of what direction our current society is heading in, the destination God calls us to is the same yesterday, today, and tomorrow.

There is that universal call to oneness with God that beckons us and continues to tug at our hearts, even during all the noise, distractions, and strong currents pulling us in the wrong directions. The call to know God is something that echoes deep in our hearts that even today, amidst all the societal changes—and no matter how far humankind wants to distance ourselves from God—we are drawn to continue to seek it.

As Saint Augustine said, "You have made us o Lord and our hearts will not rest until it rests in you." It starts with that call to know and to love God that empowers us to respond and become leaders. It is that timeless and transcendent call that motivates us and inspires us to lead and arouse passion and enthusiasm. It is the same call that tugged at Saint Augustine, Saint Francis, Mother Teresa, Padre Pio, and Pope John Paul II. In that call is the love of God that keeps on knocking on the door of our hearts, wanting to reach out to all of us, no matter what time, no matter what century. That moment when we open that door is when we will realize that God's love overflows. The love of God is so strong in us that we become so inspired to want to share the love of God, extend it, and let everyone else know about the love of God. It is that love that motivates and inspires us to answer that call and to lead others to do the same so that they will know that God's love is also for them and that we all share the same destiny of oneness with God. We are drawn to respond to God's timeless call, and so we reach up, but we are also drawn to share that call with others, and so we reach for the hands of our brothers and sisters.

> Late have I loved You, beauty so old and so new: late have I loved You. And see, You were within and I was in the external world and sought You there, and in my unlovely state I plunged into those lovely created things which You made. You were with me, and I was not with You. The lovely things kept me far from You, though if they did not have their existence in You, they had no existence at all. You called and cried out loud and shattered my deafness. You were radiant and resplendent, You put to flight my blindness. You were fragrant, and I drew in my breath and now pant after You. I tasted you, and I feel but hunger and thirst for You. You touched me, and am set on fire to attain the peace which is Yours.
>
> —Saint Augustine

God's Vineyard Today

Part of trying to understand leaders and leadership in today's context is the need to understand not only society but its people, the followers who will be led, and from where leadership will emerge. In other words, we need to have an understanding of who is being led and know that they are also the talent pool for the next generation of leaders.

One approach to understanding the people and their worldview is by using the sociological approach of examining the generations. Generational analysis has a distinguished place in the social sciences; and when it comes to understanding the generations' distinct characteristics and values, there is no shortage of research data. Just in the last fifty-plus years, there has been extensive research on the different generations that are now coexisting and intermingling with one another. And we have learned a great deal about ourselves, the generations we belong to, and the generations around us. We have come to understand that there are certain societal elements that have distinctly shaped each generation. We have come to know that each generation has been shaped by their environments and that each generation holds unique sets of values.

In the workplace, where much of this generational research is happening, for example, baby boomers value experience, optimism, and the expectation to work longer hours in exchange for more money;[37] members of Generation X prefer stability[38] and millennials seek meaning in their work.[39] Research on the generational dynamics has ramped up because all four generations are now so interconnected, particularly in today's workforce, yet with very distinct priorities and needs.

These generations are also distinctly shaped by the leadership models that they are used to. My generation has spent some of our formative years witnessing leadership figures such as Pope John Paul II, President Bill Clinton, Microsoft founder and CEO Bill Gates, and Mother Teresa. These were some of the prominent leaders impressed in the minds of my generation. Subconsciously or consciously, they are our leadership models. Personally, for me, growing up in the '80s and the '90s, Pope John Paul II and Mother Teresa are two of my generation's remarkable leaders that had a

---

[37] J. Gilbert, "The Millennials: A New Generation of Employees, and New Set of Engagement Policies," *The Workplace* (September/October 2011).

[38] A. Levenson, "Millennials and the World of Work: An Economist's Perspective," *Journal of Business and Psychology*, 25(2), 257.

[39] N.M. Schullery, "Workplace Engagement and Generational Differences in Values," *Business Communication Quarterly*, 76(2), 252.

strong and lasting influence on me. They responded to their call faithfully and with humility and with love. They saw the needs of the people of God, and they stepped up to serve and to lead. They were authentic in their actions, and that captivated a lot of young followers like me. They have set the foundation for the next generation of leaders.

> *I do not pray for success. I pray for faithfulness.*
>
> —Mother Teresa

The next generation in line to fill leadership roles are the millennials, and many of them are actually serving as leaders now. And this generational group is the largest. If you think the baby boomer generation is big, think again. There are 76 million baby boomers, 51 million Generation Xers, and 87 million millennials. Some consider the millennials to be the next greatest generation. They have already surpassed the baby boomers in terms of population size, and so, due to their size and other overwhelming factors, they are projected to have a significant impact on this world today and in the future. They have already started to become adults and are now entering the workplace in droves and filling leadership roles already. And for the majority of their group, they are the ones being developed to lead some of our companies and organizations in the near future. Many are, in fact, already leaders at their companies. According to the Millennial Leadership Study, 91 percent of the 412 millennials they surveyed aspire to be a leader, so there is no doubt that leadership is important to this generation. The millennials are the future of leadership, and they embody many of the shifts in the way we think about leadership today. It would be worth our time to take a look at how this generation views leadership—both their current leadership and their ideal future leadership—what they expect from their leaders, and what they themselves might look like as leaders.

Sadly, research shows that the millennials are leaving the Church in droves. A 2015 study by Pew Research found that fewer and fewer millennials identify with any religion at all here in the United States. And so, how relevant are the stories of the saints today? And would it still be possible to find in today's world the likes of Saint Francis or Mother Teresa, who can lead and inspire the generations of the postmodern world? And if someone like Saint Francis or Mother Teresa were to emerge as a leader, how would he or she be viewed as a leader? What would we expect from him or her?

Leader for God's Vineyard Today

Amidst all of these changes and complexities we are now witnessing, I feel that we are tremendously blessed to have Pope Francis, who chose the name Francis after the saint from Assisi, emerge to be the leader of our church today. He is a great, exemplary leader for many of today's youth. His emergence is very timely, and the church undoubtedly needs that kind of leadership right now. Saint Francis of Assisi also lived during a time of dramatic change. At San Damiano, Saint Francis heard the call from God to rebuild His church, which was falling into ruins. Saint Francis took the message to heart, took it literally, and responded by physically rebuilding and renovating the abandoned and run-down church one stone at a time with his own hands. He would eventually realize that the message was actually a call to rebuild the spiritual church, the universal church, which was suffering from various scandals, corruption, heresies, immoralities, and loss of faith.

Pope Francis, in so many ways, is also called to rebuild God's holy church. And again, it is not the rebuilding of the physical church, not the brick and mortar structure of the church, but the spiritual church. Scandals, immoralities, and heresies are not new to the church today. Pope Francis is called to repair and renew the universal church from the multiple crises it has encountered in the last several years. It is in the midst of a crisis where we find great leaders step up, step forward, and face the challenge to reform, rebuild, and renew the Church and its faithful. Pope Francis, after the model of Saint Francis of Assisi, is the kind of leader to see us through these tough times.

The past several years have been a particularly delicate time for the Catholic Church. Catholics and the rest of the world are still reeling from the terrible scandals that have rocked the church in recent decades. There's the sexual abuse scandal; there's the issue of homosexuality; there's the issue of celibacy in the priesthood; there's the problem of financial scandals. This boat keeps getting rocked by one powerful wave after another, and the faithful keep getting tossed around and about. Many Catholics are losing faith and are leaving the church in droves. According to a 2014 Pew Research study, the number of Catholics in the United States have dropped by almost 4 percent since 2007.[40] People are still converting to the church, and that is not new, but according to Pew, for every one convert, more than six Catholics leave the church. The pope definitely has his work cut out for him. We're still in stormy seas in a boat getting rocked by strong waves, but many of us place our trust and belief in the leadership that we have at the helm to see us through.

He is a leader we can trust because people see him as a humble man who places others above himself. One of the things that stand out with Pope Francis is his humble request for prayers from everyone he meets. When he visited the United States in 2015, you could hear his prayer request over and over again, asking everyone he met to pray for him. If his visit to the United States were a song, "Pray for me" would be the refrain line. We usually don't expect to hear a powerful world leader make such a humble request from

---

[40] Pew Research Center. *2014 Religious Landscape Study.*

us laypeople; it is usually the other way around. We usually expect church leaders to be the ones interceding for their people, but this gesture shows that we are all in this together with him. He shows us that our prayers count just as much, and that he needs his flock to pray for him as well. That small request signifies to us that he, as our pope, is just as human as we all are and that we are just as close to God as he is. It shows his vulnerability. And that is okay. It is okay for leaders to show their humanity and their vulnerability. Leaders often try to show their strong and powerful side, never their weak side, but people connect to leaders who show the more human side of their leadership.

And then there's his humility and simplicity. One of the popular topics that the media brought up during the Pope's visit regarded the old, plain, and worn-out black shoes of the Pope. Well, the media was not necessarily watching and criticizing the fashion style of the Pope, but instead, they were pointing out his modesty. Since the sixteenth century, popes have typically worn handmade red satin shoes embroidered with gold thread. So his departure from the fancy red shoes is a small, almost unnoticeable symbol of the style of Pope Francis, but it is yet another profound symbol of his leadership that is about simplicity and humility. And people noticed. When you are in a leadership position, everything gets noticed. People can detect even small acts, and they can have a significant impact on them.

Some observers were surprised by his humble actions and ways, but it is no surprise to many who knew him as archbishop in Argentina. Popes usually live in the large, beautiful, and Renaissance-decorated third-floor of the Apostolic Palace, with a view that is overlooking Saint Peter's Square, but after his election, Pope Francis refused to live there. Instead, he chose to live in a modest three-room flat called Saint Martha's House located behind a gas station. Here is where Pope Francis dines with the cardinals and other clergy guests of the Vatican.

On the night of his election, he was known to have skipped

Lessons in Leadership from the Saints

the papal limousine in favor of riding the bus with his fellow cardinals. This simplicity and modesty is what he is used to as the archbishop of Buenos Aires. In his earlier days as a priest and even as archbishop, he would ride public transportation to get around so he could be with the people, so that he could hear their concerns, and so that he could minister to the neediest.

He truly is the Pope of the people. He is always trying to be with the people. It is through these seemingly insignificant and small gestures and actions that he preaches to us quietly. He is preaching not by words, but by his actions, which in reality speak louder than words. It is invigorating to see our Pope, the leader of the Catholic Church, the Vicar of Christ, authentically living out the examples of Christ. His actions say it all. No matter what generational background you come from and no matter what leadership style you are used to, you have to be moved by such an example. It is encouraging and inspiring to see that we have a leader who is there to serve the people, to serve the flock that he leads, to serve the poor and the neediest—a leader that fits the current times so perfectly.

> *O God, who, through the merits of blessed Francis,*
> *didst give increase to Thy Church, by*
> *enriching her with new offspring:*
> *Grant us that following his example*
> *we may despise earthly goods*
> *and ever rejoice in partaking of Thy heavenly gifts.*
> *Through our Lord Jesus Christ, Thy Son,*
> *Who lives and reigns with You and Holy*
> *Spirit, one God, forever, and ever.*
> *Amen.*[41]

---

[41] Prayer and devotion retrieved from www.EWTN.com.

BECOMING A LEADER, BECOMING A SAINT

Diversity in Leadership

> *How monotonously alike all the great tyrants and conquerors have been; how gloriously different are the saints.*
>
> —C. S. Lewis [42]

In today's complex and diverse society, we have seen leaders come from all walks of life. From presidents to CEOs to athletes to religious leaders, we have seen some great examples of what leadership is and what it should look like. There is a leadership model for each and every person, and there is a leadership model for each and every situation. There are certain brands of leadership that fit with certain situational and organizational demands. A General Patton kind of leader would probably make sense in certain wartime situations but would probably not make a very effective religious organization leader. A religious leader might not be an effective leader in a Fortune 500 company with very

---

[42] C. S. Lewis, *Mere Christianity* (New York: Touchstone, 1996), pp 190–191.

demanding, high-profile shareholders who want to make sure their portfolio grows ten-fold in the next ten weeks.

There is an ideal leadership for every situation. There has to be a fit between the leader and the organization. And we have to recognize that leaders come in different sizes, shapes, and forms. Some are loud. Some are subdued and analytical. Some are authoritative. Some are more of a servant. Some are humble. Some emphasize service. Some are hands-on. Some are more action oriented. Some are extroverts. Some are thinkers. Some are introverts.

Over the last few years, we have seen an increase in the realization that there is something about quiet leadership. We have seen an increase in the research on how some of our working situations now call for a more quiet leadership. Leadership in the past, especially with the leadership trend rooted in the Industrial Revolution, was seen more as a role for someone who is dominant, charismatic, bold, assertive, and loud. We placed a heavy emphasis on leaders who were particularly vocal. But now, in our postmodern era and in a knowledge economy where there is more emphasis on creativity and proactivity among members and individual contributors, the emerging kind of leadership, according to a number of scholars, is quiet leadership. In the technology world of work, leaders probably would want to let their software developers do their thing and do their job autonomously and stop directing. We want leadership to let professionals be the professionals that they are and do what they do. We live in a different kind of work environment now, and we have to recognize the shift in the tone of leadership. One of the leading scholars on this quiet revolution is Susan Cain. She authored the 2012 nonfiction bestseller *Quiet: The Power of Introverts in a World that Can't Stop Talking*. We are now in a knowledge economy where individual contributors are more empowered, more informed, and more highly educated. We believe that each and every member has something important and something unique to contribute. Some argue that our milieu is ripe for quiet leadership because such leadership allows for smoother facilitation of creative ideas. In a flatter world, we don't need to tell everyone what to do. It is quite a shift from the Industrial Age when groups were more hierarchical and people were more restricted, disempowered, and were told what to do. People in the past relied heavily on leadership for directions. But now, especially with the rise of knowledge workers and teams where people are more self-managing, there has to be more room for a leadership that includes a more introverted style with fewer directives.

Research by Adam Grant of the University of Pennsylvania, Francesca Gino of Harvard University, and David Hoffman of the University of North Carolina suggests that both introverted and extroverted leadership can be equally effective, but with different kinds of people.[43] It does make sense in the many social settings we are in for one personality to make way for another. It is likely for one characteristic to complement the other, for introverts to complement the extroverts, and for extroverts to complement the introverts. It is like the yin and yang in action. Leaders who can discern the situational demands and who can adapt to those demands and play the appropriate role can be effective leaders. Sometimes, depending on the situation, leaders need to be the Joan of Arc type of leader, an outspoken, frontal-attack, war leader; but sometimes, leaders need to also be like Saint John the Silent of the sixth century and be contemplative and quiet so that they can take the time to absorb, discern, and prayerfully reflect on the situation.

Leaders must be able to find that balance and play the role as demanded by the situation. Leaders must be able to do some

---

[43] Adam M. Grant, Francesca Gino, & David A. Hoffman, "Reversing the Extraverted Leadership Advantage: The Role of Employee Proactivity," *Academy of Management Journal*, 54, 3 (2011), 528–550.

introspection, take stock of the situation, gather the wisdom of the crowds, and then lead the way.

As Stephen Covey recommended in his book, *Seven Habits of Highly Effective People*, leaders must be able to listen quietly with the intent to understand and not listen with the intent to reply. In a world that was described by author Susan Cain as a world that cannot stop talking, there are so many people trying to get their voices heard. Too many people talking and very few people listening just opens up the likelihood for more misunderstandings. We live in a very polarized world because people don't take the effort and the time to listen. We seem to have lost the art of listening. As leaders, we have to learn how to listen to others and listen with the intent to hear their points of view. We need to learn how to be quiet, open up our minds, absorb the situation, and seek to understand. We need to learn to be fully present and listen, not only to one another, but to God.

> *What we need most in order to make progress is to be silent before this great God with our appetite and with our tongue, for the language He best hears is silent love.*
>
> —Saint John of the Cross

Whether an introvert or an extrovert, a leader must be able to find the right balance. You must be able to sit quietly and listen to the voice of God in silence for, as Saint Faustina wrote: "God works in a silent soul without hindrance." Be not afraid of silence. Too often, we feel the need to fill in moments of silence and stillness with sound, sometimes noise. We're just not used to silence anymore. We get uncomfortable when things go silent. But we must learn to seek out moments of silence and use those moments to hear God's message. Let's also learn to use silence to proclaim God's message for sometimes the silence of our hearts speak louder than our voice. And whether you are an introvert or an extrovert, you must also be able to go out and loudly proclaim the love of God. That does not necessarily mean preaching with words. There is the saying that I am sure many of you have heard that is attributed to Saint Francis of Assisi: "Preach the gospel, and if necessary, use words." We might not have the preaching eloquence of Saint Anthony or the peaceful persuasiveness of Saint Dominic, but we can still proclaim the love of God through our actions. And in this day and age, preaching through action is the way to go.

In fact, it is often more effective to get your message across by your actions rather than by your words. Mother Teresa of Calcutta, for instance, was able to preach the love of God not as a loud preacher but by her quiet and authentic actions. She converted a lot of hearts without saying much vocally. She didn't have to say much because people witnessed and felt God's love through her actions. Her actions were definitely louder than her words. She was like a quiet river that meandered peacefully to its destination, giving life to everything that it touched—the plants, the trees, and the fish. There is something peaceful about this river, and people just want to follow it and ride it down, for they know that it will lead to something greater. The serene flow of the quiet river is easy to follow, unlike the loud, raging river. The loud, raging river flows violently and unpredictably, carving out the path before it like a bully and disregarding the life that depends on it. Mother Teresa transformed lives not by boisterousness but by her humble, quiet deeds.

Quiet Leadership

There is something about quiet leadership that people just want to follow. Take Thomas Malcolm Muggeridge, the journalist who introduced Mother Teresa to the world, for example. He was a renowned cynic and agnostic prior to meeting Mother Teresa. He went to Calcutta intent on questioning the true motivations of Mother Teresa, but after meeting her and witnessing her selfless love and dedication to the poor and the destitute, he came out convinced and transformed. He eventually converted all because of what he had witnessed in the acts of Mother Teresa. Mother Teresa preached to Muggeridge about God's love through her quiet acts of love for God's poor.

And that is the kind of preaching we need these days. Although the Christian mission of preaching to the ends of the earth is far from completion, most people today have probably heard about Jesus and the gospel already. And yet, despite the knowledge of Christ and His messages, many people are still unmoved and transformed. Some people are even repelled. Karl Rahner, a Jesuit theologian of the twentieth century said, "The number one cause of atheism is Christians. Those who proclaim Him with their mouths and deny Him with their actions is what an unbelieving world finds unbelievable." And that is why, in an unbelieving world, we find the likes of Mahatma Gandhi, Mother Teresa, and Saint Francis highly admirable and appealing because they were genuinely faithful; the ways they lived their lives are authentic testaments to their beliefs.

Christians going around proclaiming the Word of God would have to consider other innovative ways to preach effectively. We need to learn from the timeless wisdom of the saints. Preaching does not always have to be done so with words. Some of the most convincingly holy people who I find truly respectable and inspiring are not always the ones out in the pulpit or on TV vocally preaching the gospel. Some of the most admirable Christians are the ones I see praying quietly, humbly, and genuinely in the back of the church, where no one is watching, or those Christians who go out day in and day out to live out their faith with steadfastness and in service of God and others, and never waiting for accolades. They do not tell others what they should do, but through their quiet deeds of holiness, they inspire others to action. As Saint Benedict of Nursia said, "He should first show them in deeds rather than words all that is good and holy."[44] Just like what the old adage says, "Be the change that you want to see." Many Christians aspire to change the world and make it a better place, but we have to recognize that no matter how much we want to preach to others, the change must start with us. Let our actions speak and preach for us.

Consider another quiet example, that of Saint Alphonsus Liguori. He had an early start in being inspirational in his deeds. As a young, pious teenager, he was living out his Christian beliefs in his own quiet, daily ways. One day, one of the non-Christian slaves selected to wait upon him fervently expressed his desire to be baptized into the same Catholic faith as young Alphonsus. And when asked why he wanted to convert to Christianity, he replied, "The example of my young master has made a great impression on me; for it is impossible that that religion can be false, which makes him lead a life so pure and holy."[45] Little did young Alphonsus know that his daily actions were actually *preaching* to this man.

Influencing others is done best not necessarily by voice, but by everyday good deeds and by living out real-life examples. In leadership studies, one of the best predictors of leadership influence is how the leader's behavior serves as a model. How leaders behave and act can have a profound influence on followers. People nowadays are more inclined to follow examples of leaders rather

---

[44] *The Rule of Saint Benedict* (translated) (Mineola, NY: Dover Publications), p.5.

[45] *The Life of Saint Alphonsus Maria De Liguori* by one of the Redemptorist Fathers (Baltimore: John Murphy & Co, 1855), p.23.

than follow their directions. We live in a very informed society, and we do not particularly like it when we get told by someone else what to do, especially when we can easily figure things out on our own. We get our motivations to act by inspiration. The actions of others rather than verbal commands are what spur us into action. Actions speak louder than words. A leader's positive influence—and it doesn't always have to be vocalized—is what keeps the followers engaged, motivated, happy, and productive.

Jesus Christ, our leader, suffered quietly and only spoke seven last words as He died on the cross. And yet, this quiet gesture spurred into action millions of Christians. What could speak louder than the words, "Greater love has no one than this: to lay down one's life for one's friends" (John 15:13) than the actual action itself.

How the saints lived out their faith and their convictions inspires a lot of followers time and time again. Their leadership, by their real-life examples—even though they are from a different time—are worth another look, especially now as we search for leadership models that actually work. The way the saints manifested their leadership in their lives, both internally and externally, are some of the best and most effective examples we have for how to influence, how to evangelize, and how to preach the love of God.

> *The fruit of silence is prayer. The fruit of prayer is faith. The fruit of faith is love. The fruit of love is service. The fruit of service is peace.*
>
> —Mother Teresa

Going back to the example of Saint Francis of Assisi, in the thirteenth century, right in the middle of the Crusades, times were very unstable, very bloody and very hostile for Christians and Muslims. Francis, being the peace-loving friar that he was, wanted the fighting to end. He decided to go to Egypt with the hopes of converting the sultan of Egypt, Malik-al-Kamil, to Christianity. He was going to risk his life and talk with the sultan personally; he was prepared to die and be a martyr for the faith. His bravery paid off because they actually ended up having a peaceful encounter. Both Francis and the sultan gained a new perspective on one another, and they both found new respect for each other's faith and culture.

We need to seek first to understand, then to be understood second. Stephen Covey (1932–2012) wrote in his bestseller book, *Seven Habits of Highly Effective People*, "Seek first to understand, then to be understood." It is a timeless and proven principle that is practiced by highly effective people. It is a principle that many attribute to Saint Francis of Assisi because he lived it out even in the toughest of all situations. In the midst of all the misunderstandings and turmoil between Christians and Muslims, Saint Francis made the effort to first seek to understand the sultan rather than to be understood. And because of Francis's humble way of approaching the sultan, the sultan was pleased, and he got along with Francis and his companions. It is because of their relationship that, even to this day, we still see Franciscans in the Holy Land. The Franciscans were permitted to have a custodian priory in the Holy Land, and today, that is still the case, even eight hundred years after Francis's visit with the sultan.

This is just the type of approach that we need to have in our relationships with one another today. Look around in today's world. There are so many divisions and so many polarized opinions because we seem to have forgotten how to really listen. We live "in a world that can't stop talking," and when people choose to listen, they tend to listen with the intent to reply. We need to learn and practice how to listen with the intent to understand. As leaders, we have to be able to listen to our people, to our constituents, and even to our critics and our competitors. We have to listen to understand and really know where they are coming from. We need to empathize and put ourselves in their shoes because their feelings, thoughts, and beliefs are just as real as ours and are worthy of consideration. We need to learn to share not only their joy but their sufferings and frustrations. We need to remember that as Christians called to lead, we represent Christ's love and concern for every single person, and we need to hear them out.

Strategic, Tactical, Agile, Adaptive

In the literature on leadership, one of the main important points of emphasis, especially in this day and age, is on strategic leadership. Strategic thinking is a key and imperative leadership characteristic that people and organizations look for in their leaders. We live in a world that is in a state of constant change—changes in technology, economy, attitudes, cultural values, and morals. There is a demand for leaders, for organizations, and for individuals to have the ability to anticipate, adapt, and deal successfully with change and challenges. Leaders must have the ability to think strategically in order to keep the mission moving forward in fulfilling its purpose. They must be able to deal with cross-cultural dynamics and diversity and even be able to leverage those factors to achieve organizational success. They have to be able to get a diverse group of individuals to buy into a common vision. They have to be able to challenge their own assumptions and welcome divergent points of view. They have to be able to detect ambiguous threats as well as opportunities.

Leaders must learn from mistakes. They must be able to acknowledge their mistakes and make the necessary corrections and improvements. They adapt and they thrive in the midst of all the complexities. Even in times of failure, they find a way to bounce right back.

> *An intelligent mind is simple and teachable;
> it sees its faults and allows itself to be guided.
> A mind that is dull and narrow never sees its
> faults even when shown them. It is always
> pleased with itself and never learns to do right.*
>
> —*Saint Teresa of Avila*

Leadership is demanding. Leaders continually face many tough challenges. And these challenges are not new and isolated to today's business world. These leadership challenges we see today are some of the same challenges that were faced by saints in the past as well. Again, we need to look no further for leadership models that we can learn from in order to navigate some of these challenges we have today. The saints demonstrated authentic and genuine leadership choices and, at the same time, some of the most authentic ways for pleasing God.

Saint Francis Xavier on Leadership

In the 1500s, Europe was going through a period of many changes. It was the height of the Renaissance. It was the European age of exploration and expansion and scientific discoveries. They were discovering new worlds and encountering new cultures in different parts of the world. Just before the turn of the century, Columbus had discovered the New World. And as you can imagine, just like in today's Information Age, the people of the 1500s were also getting bombarded with a lot of new information; much of it was drastic and dramatic. In a period of change, many of the old ways of thinking and doing are likely to get rocked, questioned, and changed. It was a time, just like today, that would call for leaders to be strategic in order to manage change effectively and to adapt and survive.

For the Jesuits, who had just started to form in the early half of 1500's, it was a very busy time. In 1540, the same year the Jesuits were officially approved by Pope Paul III as a religious order, King John of Portugal had asked Ignatius for missionaries to spread the Christian faith to the new Portuguese territories in Asia. With a young and bustling religious order that had many of its new members already preoccupied with spreading the gospel in other distant lands, Saint Ignatius had no one else left to send to Asia but Francis Xavier. Not a bad last choice at all because Francis Xavier, who would later become a saint, would be the first ever Jesuit missionary and, along with Saint Therese of Lisieux, co-patron saint of foreign missions. He would also later be considered one of the greatest missionaries after Saint Paul. And for leaders dealing with global diversity and cross-cultural interactions, Saint Francis Xavier might be able to show us a few real-world examples.

Europe and the missionaries knew very little about the new lands. Remember, this was the 1500s, the age of exploration, and Europe was just learning about these newly discovered lands and cultures. Francis Xavier's great ambition of bringing God to the world was not going to be an easy task at all. In this journey upon which he was embarking, he was a pioneer and had to start from scratch. There were no templates for how to do mission work in those lands, and so he had to figure things out on his own. He had to learn the language and the culture—not only once but several times as he experienced the diversity of cultures as he went from island to island and country to country.

He encountered many challenges and difficulties in his missionary trips, but he learned quickly. As he went from one culture to another, he had to be agile and flexible. Being agile and flexible are important leadership qualities that we consider of high value in today's society, particularly because of the complexities and the continuously changing environment we are in. Along with being able to adapt to change, another valuable and complementary quality that a leader must have is being able to work well with people from other cultures. Francis Xavier, in his own strategic and prayerful ways, demonstrated these leadership qualities, and we would greatly benefit from his examples.

As Europe began to expand and encounter new cultures, an effective leader had to recognize how to work with people from other cultures just as today's society emphasizes requiring its leaders, in our highly globalized environment, to have the ability to work with people from diverse backgrounds. Saint Francis Xavier's pioneering work with other cultures demonstrated the importance of these leadership qualities. He adapted to the situations that he faced, and he worked well with people who were very different from him.

Francis Xavier went to Asia to evangelize and spread the message of the gospel. In the 1500s, this was not an easy task. It's not any easier today, but it's an even more difficult task in the late Medieval period. Unlike today, they did not have textbooks or videos about other cultures. There were no travel brochures or anything. Nowadays, we can find out anything and everything about the details of our next trip online. The missionary work that Francis Xavier did was truly pioneering work. Some of the people he was working with were not welcoming and were even hostile to the Europeans. The situation called for a strategy, and Saint Francis Xavier, through prayer and through his imitation of Christ, had his own strategic response. I do not think it was an intentionally well-crafted strategic response similar to how we think of strategies in today's business world, but it was nonetheless strategic. It must have been the guidance of Divine wisdom and the discerning and prayerful attitude of Francis Xavier that made his actions seem so well-crafted and strategic.

His was an approach that started with humility. Having been sent directly by King John, with the Pope's blessing, he could have been the most powerful European in the East, and he could have

Lessons in Leadership from the Saints

easily taken advantage of such authority. But in his humility, he did not desire such power nor did he use that to his advantage. He was supposed to live in the comfortable quarters of the bishop's palace, but he declined; instead, he set up camp at a local hospital for the incurables. There, he lived with the locals who were sick; he cared for them, he washed their wounds, and he attended to their needs. These acts of humility and servanthood also allowed him to get to know the locals better and earn their trust. He was able to understand their needs, both physical and spiritual. And because he lived closely with the people he was evangelizing to and serving, he heard and saw first-hand the needs of the local people. He personally gathered all the data that he could, which then enabled him to come up with a plan to help them, to educate them, to enrich them, and to bring them the good news of the Christian faith. For Saint Francis Xavier, conversation preceded conversion. And this was key to his success as a missionary and as a leader. He had earned the trust of the local villagers. He had to first know the people he was serving, connect with them, and genuinely understand their culture, their values, and their needs. As a leader, he was able to cultivate a culture and an environment of trust, where it showed that he was committed to them.

> *As soon as I arrived on this coast, I sought to learn from them what they knew about Christ our Lord.* [46]

The Portuguese had been in Goa for thirty years already before Francis Xavier arrived, and what he found out first-hand as he was working with the locals was that the people of Goa were baptized simply to please the Portuguese. And so, to put Francis Xavier's leadership approach in a language some of us might use in today's business world, Francis Xavier first had to

---

[46] Letter 20, To Xavier's companions living in Rome, from Cochin, India, January 15, 1544.

do a "needs assessment" of the people before committing to any action planning. He realized that many of the other missionaries in Asia failed to convert the natives to Christianity because they did not have a missionary who was concerned with such pious and holy matters. They got baptized, but they were not instructed in the essence of the faith. The other missionaries failed because they simply wanted to proselytize them into European Christianity. But for Francis Xavier, he had to first understand what the needs of the people were. His genuine care for the people enabled him to understand the value of first gaining the people's trust. According to a recent social science research by Susan Fiske, Amy Cuddy, and Peter Glick, one of the first things a person does when he or she meets another person for the first time is to try to figure out whether they can trust that person or not.[47] It's instinctive for people to do so. People will evaluate others of their trustworthiness and authenticity. And for a European missionary coming into a completely new land to deliver the good news of the gospel, gaining the people's trust is a must.

Francis Xavier's approach of first gaining the people's trust and mingling with them allowed him to deploy other effective strategies in his evangelization. He was able to take stock of what they already knew about Christ and how their culture operated. He was able to gather the information necessary to move forward with his evangelization mission. His "data-gathering" enabled him to have an "information-based" approach to his evangelization.

Now, remember that all these strategies and methodologies were occurring during a time before we had the formal academic leadership studies that we do today. Nonetheless, Francis Xavier had deployed some of the most effective leadership methods in his evangelization. In addition to his very strategic approach in

---

[47] Susan T. Fiske, Amy J.C. Cuddy, & Peter Glick. "Universal dimensions of social cognition: Warmth and competence." *Trends in Cognitive Science*, Vol.11 No.2.

Lessons in Leadership from the Saints

his evangelization mission, he also deployed some creativity to get around the difficulties and the challenges that came with the mission. When he first arrived in India, Francis Xavier did not know the local language, so he had to come up with a creative way to evangelize and teach the locals about the Christian faith. Well, after hanging out with the native people for a while, he discovered that the local Indian people loved music. With that information, he then set up on a street corner with some Christian images behind him and a bell in his hand, and he would start singing catchy and rhyming jingles with a message about Christ. Through his singing and performance, he would attract the local villagers, mostly children. He would then teach them catechism with simple catchy songs. And the children would repeat the songs and sing them back to their family members. The songs and, more important, the message of the songs, would catch on with the rest of the villagers. This is how he started teaching and spreading the gospel to the thousands of villagers in India.

With his work at the local hospital and his singing acts on the streets, he was able to build rapport with the local people, which in turn enabled him to effectively spread the message of Christ to the people of Goa. As a leader, he knew how to work with people around him, and he surrounded himself with the right people to help him evangelize and translate the language. He knew from the beginning that the harvest is plenty but the laborers are few, so he started by educating the people who surrounded him. He had also anticipated that Christianity in Goa would not be perpetuated if they did not remain there, and so he devised a strategy to first train and educate the local native clergy. He is often credited in missionary work for instilling the belief of first educating the local native clergy not only as a way to help fulfill the current mission and vision, but also as a way to ensure that Christianity's roots get firmly established so that it lasts for generations. This was a strategy that allowed him to build a strong foundation for Christianity to flourish in Goa. He created a missionary culture in

Goa where people and missionaries are connected and committed to one another.

In leadership studies today, we know that great leaders surround themselves with people who are smarter and more experienced than themselves in areas where they might have their own gaps. Francis Xavier exemplified this even before there was such thing as leadership studies. He recognized and engaged the strengths of others. As an effective leader, he went to the experts around him. He found translators not only to help him with translating the language, but he educated them first so that they would understand the message of Christianity. With the translators he first educated, he was able to get help preaching in public and in private homes. And as a model of leadership, you will see the Francis Xavier recognized the importance of building relationships. He was able to get over the communication and cultural roadblocks and reach out to the children, to the slaves, to the abandoned, and to the sick. Despite the language difficulties, he was able to create an environment of open communication and trust that facilitated the smooth transmission of God's word and wisdom to the people of Goa. However, he was not just communicating or preaching the Word of God to the people. He actually showed genuine charitable concerns for their souls. People are good at detecting genuineness. The villagers of Goa saw Francis Xavier's authenticity and genuineness right when he arrived, and they were attracted to that. He had no problem living with the poor and the sick. With the evangelical poverty that he learned from Ignatius, from Saint Francis of Assisi, and other Christians who had gone before him who embraced the poverty and humility taught by Christ, Francis Xavier was able to relate to the people of Goa. And with his genuine leadership qualities, his tactical evangelization, and his prayerful discernment of God's will, he became quite successful in his mission. All of Goa was converted in a matter of half a year.

Those humble gestures by Francis Xavier were not intended

to simply be a teaching case for business schools about strategy. I doubt that he intended to have such a strategy in the first place—at least not in the sense that we think of strategy in today's business context. He was simply living out his missionary vows and his Christian values. His strategies genuinely stemmed from his values and from his thoughtful prayers, leading him to act and serve the people with humility.

It is quite a noble thing to see leaders do this in today's business environment. Getting down to the level of the people you serve and spending time with them is a leadership strategy that can be truly effective, leading to remarkable results. The better you understand the people, the better you will be able to relate to them and allow them to relate to you. That just makes good business sense. However, Francis Xavier's actions of getting to know the people better were not done as a means to an end. It was not a business move. He genuinely cared for the people, and it showed. He reached out with genuine compassion for the poor and sick people he served. And it was by his sincerity and authenticity that he was able to establish the foundation for a trusting and open relationship. His strategy was effective for leadership and enabled him to build a rapport and establish trusting relationships.

Mother Teresa, a missionary just like Saint Francis Xavier, had a similar approach when she was first getting started out in Calcutta. Again, I doubt that she was intentionally deploying a strategy in the sense that we define strategy nowadays but, like Saint Francis Xavier, she was very effective in being able to reach out to the people.

Mother Teresa grew up in a relatively comfortable home and could have stayed there with her family, but instead, having that true missionary spirit like Saint Francis Xavier, she left it all so that she could bring hope and comfort to the poorest of the poor. When she was working in Calcutta, she made the effort to connect with the poor by making her home with them. She even dressed like them. She changed the way she dressed, from her religious habit to the white Indian sari, out of respect for the traditional Indian dress that the local women were wearing. It was one of her ways to be one with the people. She felt that it was important that she mix with the people and show oneness with the people she was serving.

> *But you will receive power when the Holy Spirit comes on you; and you will be my witnesses in Jerusalem, and in all Judea and Samaria, and to the ends of the earth.*
>
> *—Acts 1:8*

The Church has always been missionary, right from the very beginning. The message of Christ in the New Testament empowers the likes of Mother Teresa and Francis Xavier to spread the Good News to all the ends of the earth. Missionary work is a must for us Christians, but it is not an easily understood task, nor is it an easy task at all. It takes dedication, lots of prayers, perseverance, open-mindedness, and strategic thinking. The pioneering work of Francis Xavier and Mother Teresa in missionary work lays out some good examples, not only for current and future missionary workers, but for all of us in our dealings with others and particularly our dealings with one another in this highly globalized and multicultural society. Francis Xavier and Mother Teresa reached out to the people they served by getting to know them and even by being one with them. They adapted to the customs and the language of the people. I do not think that Mother Teresa and Francis Xavier were being intentionally strategic. They were discerning. Their strategies were guided by their prayers and their drive to do God's will. Their strategies were unassumingly fueled by their Christian values and their humility and utter respect for humanity.

If their stories of humility, genuine caring, and their approach to building relationships all sound familiar, it is because they come from a story that we Christians are very familiar with. It is the story of what Jesus Christ Himself did for humanity. Jesus Christ came down from His kingdom in heaven and dwelt among us to reach us, and to even be as low as any of us so that He might lift us up. The Son of God became man so that, as the early Church Fathers Saint Irenaeus and Saint Athanasius said, we might become children of God. Francis Xavier and Mother Teresa, in their prayerful hearts, followed the footsteps of Christ and exemplified this act of Christ. They did what they had to do to lift up the people they served: the lowly and the poor. They had the ultimate example of reaching out to the people with true compassion so that they could share the Good News that they too are beloved children of God.

> *For you know the grace of our Lord Jesus Christ, that though he was rich, yet for your sake he became poor, so that you through his poverty might become rich.*
>
> *—2 Corinthians 8:9*

Strategy is a concept that is common and an absolute must in the business world; it is not typically associated with evangelization or missionary work. It might sound very businesslike to use the term *strategy*, but in order to be effective in doing the work of God today, leaders who are involved in missionary or evangelization work must also think strategically—prayerfully strategic. Especially as leaders tasked with evangelization in the modern world, we need to make sure that we consider how we send the *Good News* to others. We need to make sure our outreach strategies to our brothers and sisters are effective—that we are able to share the message of God's love and that the message is truly reaching their hearts and minds.

BJ Gonzalvo, Ph.D.

Saint Paul on Strategy and Adaptiveness

Another one of the main models of all missionaries, especially when it comes to having a strategic mindset as well as adaptability, is Saint Paul, inarguably one of the greatest Christian missionaries. Being an early Christian missionary when no one had ever heard of Christ or the gospel, Saint Paul adapted to a variety of circumstances in order to preach and spread the Good News.

Saint Paul preached far and wide. He knew that there was a lot of land to cover to reach the ends of the earth and so he had to be efficient in his preaching efforts. One of Saint Paul's strategies included preaching in the heavily populated and very diverse urban centers. He knew that everything started from the city centers, and the spread of the gospel would be more efficient if it also started from there. And so one of his main strategies as he travelled to preach was to start his efforts in the city centers. Saint Paul planted these churches in a way that facilitated the wider dispersion of the Christian faith. Christianity grew exponentially during the time of Saint Paul.

It was also in the city centers where he realized he had to adapt to the diverse populations. When Saint Paul was preaching to the Jews, he understood the importance of their use of customs and traditions and their use of history, and so he used that information to reach out to them. "When I was with the Jews, I lived like a Jew to bring the Jews to Christ. When I was with those who follow the Jewish law, I too lived under that law. Even though I am not subject to the law, I did this so I could bring to Christ who are under the law" (1 Corinthians 9:20). And when preaching to the Greeks, he understood the importance of using their reasoning and philosophy, and so he leveraged that information to appeal to them as well. Saint Paul, became all things to all men so as to win as many to Christ as possible (1 Corinthians 9:22).

The Road to Success is Not Easy

Having a strategy, however, does not mean evangelization will always lead to success and effectiveness. Leaders must also have a strategy for how to face failures, for failures are part of the reality of doing the work of God.

When Francis Xavier was in India, he deployed certain strategies that worked for the situational demands in that location. And because of the strategies he had developed for that specific situation, he had achieved quite a level of remarkable success. His strategic thinking certainly helped him convert many of the locals in Goa to Christianity. He built almost forty churches along the coast of India. Some estimates reach up to one hundred thousand baptized converts. In one of his letters back to Europe, Francis Xavier even wrote that his arms would get exhausted from baptizing the great multitudes of converts. He had quite an effective strategy that worked well in his missionary and evangelization work, but after almost three years completing his evangelization work in India, he had to move on and spread the gospel to other parts of Asia. Francis Xavier was always striving for more for God. He was deeply influenced by the founder of his religious order and his very close friend, Saint Ignatius, who was driven to perform tasks with the motto *"Ad Majorem Dei Gloriam,"* which means, "For the greater glory of God." Even today, this motto is a very important one that the Jesuits wholeheartedly carry out in many aspects of their work.

However, as Francis Xavier went on to the other parts of Asia to do more for God, the results would be different. That same level of success he had in India was not easy to replicate elsewhere. He found it especially troublesome in Japan and China. When he got to Japan, a certain failure awaited him. It was a failure that required him to rethink his strategy and use a different tactic. Japan is another culture that was utterly foreign to Francis Xavier, and so the circumstances there called for a different strategy.

The situation also needed him to first know the culture and the people because, again, he would find himself to be one of the first Europeans to arrive in that foreign land. The first time he arrived in Japan, he deployed an approach to evangelization that was similar to how he treated the people of Goa, probably thinking it would not make that big a difference. However, that same tactic did not work for the Japanese.

Embrace Failure

When Saint Francis Xavier arrived in Japan, he was dressed just like how he dressed back in Goa—in rags like a poor beggar. He embraced the same evangelical poverty that Saint Francis embraced, and so dressing like a poor man was his norm when he arrived in India. And that worked fine living with the poor in Goa. However, that evangelical poverty did not have the same appeal to the Japanese people. Japan during this time was closed to outsiders, and the villagers were hostile to foreigners. Europeans who washed ashore were seen as barbarians. And being dressed in poor beggar clothes did not help with that image. And so Francis Xavier had a tough time getting an audience with the Japanese leaders. He was rejected by the leaders as well as the people. His first attempt at evangelization in Japan was a failure, so he decided to leave.

We usually don't like this "F" word, but in today's environment, failure is part of the game. For leaders, failure is just another challenge to overcome. Leaders must learn from failures. In many of the start-up organizations today, they embrace failures. "Fail fast" as the start-up businesses like to say. Failing fast helps them to stay agile and adaptive. It helps them to identify the problem right away, find a fix, improve, and eventually have a robust product. We often see failure as bad, disgraceful, shameful, feared, and embarrassing to admit. But gritty people see failure as an opportunity. When we work at something, we strive for the good and we do our best to avoid failure, but failure happens; and when it happens, we have no choice but to accept it. Failure is an experience budding with other wonderful opportunities. Failure is like the flame that fires up resilient leaders to course-correct and seize opportunities that were previously unseen and then use that to get better.

When Francis Xavier did his missionary work in Japan, he had to face a major failure, and he had every reason in the world to simply give up and just stay in his comfort zone in Goa. But with the zeal and the passion he had for fulfilling the mission that was entrusted to him by Saint Ignatius, the Jesuits, and the Church, he chose not to despair or give up. As he was riding his ship in retreat from Japan, he prayed and reflected on what went wrong in his mission. He came to the realization that it was not the end and that that failure was just an opportunity for him to be humbled and to respect the fact that he was dealing with a different reality. That failure was giving him an opportunity to draw out the best of him and rally him to bounce back. He realized that he was dealing with a different culture and that there are some things that he would have to do or change to adapt to a culture as refined as the Japanese. He realized that it was not too late and that all he had to do was course-correct and redefine his strategy.

So he turned the ship around and resolved to adapt to the circumstances. He resolved to first understand the Japanese culture better. He learned their language and actually became fluent enough to preach in Japanese. He also recognized that the Japanese culture was a refined culture, so he changed his clothing, going from his poor beggar look to dressing handsomely in a fine cassock, surplice, and stole. He also had his companions dress in fine clothing and had them act as if they were his attendants. He presented himself to the emperor and offered him gifts as a representative of the Kingdom of Portugal. With these changes in his strategy, the emperor was pleased, and Francis Xavier would eventually be granted permission to preach to the Japanese. He would eventually become successful in baptizing many of the Japanese he encountered. He earned their respect and eventually gained an audience with Japanese leaders. He recognized the hierarchical nature of Japanese society, so in his evangelization strategy, he first talked to the leaders, established the connections there, and then preached to the rest of the village about the faith. And for Francis Xavier, conversation preceded conversion. After about two years of his strategic efforts in Japan, he was able to convert and baptize over seven hundred Japanese into Christianity. That number is much less than the one hundred thousand converts he had in India, but still, through his perseverance and strategic mindset, he overcame failure. And winning hundreds of converts for Christ is quite a remarkable feat by any standards.

We too, whether we are in a leadership position or not, need to be strategic and adaptive in our everyday tasks. There is much to learn from the saints who preceded us. We may not be doing direct missionary work like Saint Francis Xavier, but I can think of many applications of their leadership examples that we can use in our contemporary lives. In today's very complex and rapidly changing environment, we need to be constantly vigilant, constantly scanning the environment for signals of change, to anticipate potential challenges. We need to embrace change, for change is inevitable. Some of today's well-known companies thrive because of change. Leaders who are not afraid of change and are willing to go to the unknown have led some of the most successful companies that we know today. Francis Xavier could have stayed in his comfort zone, his safety zone, in Goa. But instead, he felt that there was more work to be done, and so he ventured out into unknown territory. Change came, and so did failure. These things are part of the Christian venture. But when change and failure come, we need to embrace them and accept the opportunities that come with them, for they are opportunities for us to become better Christians and better leaders.

Be Vigilant

> *Be alert and of sober mind. Your enemy the devil prowls around like a roaring lion looking for someone to devour.*
>
> —*1 Peter 5:8*

And as Saint Francis Xavier taught us, we need to have a careful assessment of the situation at all times so that we can have information we can use to devise strategies for effective leadership. Leaders must examine and diagnose the current situation and use that information to strategize. Anticipate the challenges and the roadblocks ahead, for the adversary prowls around like a roaring lion, seeking someone to devour. We need to have a strategic plan for meeting the challenges. Having a strategy is what will help us lay out the action plans for how our end goals in our Christian lives will be achieved. Having a strategy might seem counter to the whole notion of "abandonment to God's providence," but in fact, they complement one another. Just like the saying attributed to Saint Ignatius: "Pray as if everything depended on God, work as if everything depended on you."[48] A strategy enables leaders to work effectively and to foresee future consequences of the action plans as well as uncertainties and blindside hits. There are a lot of uncertainties ahead in our Christian work, but the strategic leader must be able to have a plan for adapting and getting over those challenges to ensure that we are able to see God's work through.

---

[48] Attributed to Saint Ignatius Loyola, cf. Joseph de Guibert, SJ, *The Jesuits: Their Spiritual Doctrine and Practice*, (Chicago: Loyola University Press, 1964), 148, n. 55.

> *But you, keep your head in all situations,*
> *endure hardship, do the work of an evangelist,*
> *discharge all the duties of your ministry.*
>
> *—2 Timothy 4:5*

Leadership with Humility

No matter how careful we are in our situational assessment or how good we are in our strategic planning, we have to keep in mind that our work belongs to God. Let the work we do be the work of God.

Mother Teresa and Saint Francis of Assisi constantly reminded their followers that the work they did was not theirs but God's. When asked why God picked them, they both replied that God chose them, the lowliest and the weakest, so that the people would know that what they did was possible only because of God. They wanted to make sure that it was God who got all the glory and not them.

It is not easy to find such humility these days. In today's culture of amped up self-promotion, pride, and personal horn-tooting, to want to be humble is unheard of and just plain peculiar. When was the last time you heard someone, anywhere, even from the church pulpits, preaching about humility? Humility gets a bad rap these days. Just look at how the role of humility has evolved over the years in different arenas of life, such as sports and business. One sports columnist actually wrote about humility in sports and shrewdly titled his article "May Humility Rest in Peace."[49] Being humble is just not the typical virtue promoted or practiced if one

---

[49] Patrick Hruby, *May Humility Rest in Peace*. (August 1, 2005). Accessed from www.espn.go.com on June 24, 2016.

wants to win a championship or move up the corporate ladder. We tend to associate humility with low self-esteem, shyness, lack of confidence, and an inferior sense of worth or importance. It can understandably be a very confusing conundrum, and for leaders, it can be a difficult task to find the balance between humility and self-esteem.

But despite recurring attempts to devalue the virtue of humility, new research in business actually suggests that humility is an important trait to have. In fact, some recent research studies suggest that it is one of the most important traits of a leader. According to a recent article in *Industry Week*, humility is the "number one leadership asset for 2016."[50] Humble leadership produces a number of positive outcomes for an organization. Humble leadership results in better organizational performance, more employee engagement, and higher productivity. Humble leaders are able to trump their own ego so that they can focus not on their own personal needs but on the needs of the people and of the organization. Humble leadership is exactly the type of leadership that we need in our organizations today.

It might feel like a novel concept in leadership and in business, and there are a number of articles starting to highlight it and emphasize it, but the concept of promoting the value of humility was taught long ago. Christianity has been teaching us how to be humble for over two thousand years. Jesus preached this to His disciples: "Anyone who wants to be first must be the very last, and the servant of all" (Mark 9:35).

Humility is a very foundational trait for those wishing to follow the footsteps of Christ, who came down from His kingdom in heaven to raise up the humble and the lowly. In the Old Testament, humility was a very important trait for a leader. Moses, one of the

---

[50] Industry Week. *Humility: Your Number One Leadership Asset for 2016* (January 7, 2016). Accessed from www.industryweek.com on June 20, 2016.

greatest leadership figures we have in history, was also one of the most humble in the Old Testament, "more so than any person on the face of the earth" (Numbers 12:3). Moses's humility allowed him to clearly see the purpose of God for choosing him. Because of his humility, God chose him to lead two million people out of captivity and into the promised land. In a recent homily by Pope Francis, he said, "Humility is the way to holiness." Humility clears up the murkiness brought on by too much pride and arrogance, allowing us to see our own limitations and littleness, allowing us to realize the greatness of God.

Philosophers understood humility as a meta-virtue because it serves as the foundation for all the other virtues, such as wisdom, courage, compassion, and forgiveness. As Mother Teresa said: "Humility is the mother of all virtues; purity, charity, and obedience." And as we can see, Mother Teresa lived it to the fullest. She was humble in all her endeavors, even as a leader. Her sisters and followers in the Missionaries of Charity saw this in her, and so they trusted her leadership and gave her their full support. The people also saw her genuine humility, and they too gave her a lot of support. Even as the leader of her organization, Mother Teresa still would do the lowliest work. She did the menial work just like everyone else. She was eager and happy to do whatever was needed to be done, even if it was cleaning the toilet.

Being humble leaders allows us to see what proud leaders have difficulty seeing—our limitations. As leaders, we have to recognize our limitations and weaknesses, and we need to accept that we really haven't figured it all out. We have to learn to humbly accept that we need others—our subordinates, our colleagues, our fellow brothers and sisters in Christ—to figure it all out together and know that we are in this together. We cannot accomplish God's mission all alone. We need the expertise of others. We live in a "flat world," as bestselling author, Thomas L. Friedman would say. And in a flatter world, we need to realize the value of collaboration and the value that each individual brings to the table. We need to be open, humbly open, so that we can hear from others about better methods for doing things or about things that we can improve on. We need to realize that, no matter what the task, whether it is deciding on a major acquisition or preaching to the villagers who speak a foreign language, we are all in this together. As leaders, we need to know that we need our followers just as much as they need their leader. And it is okay to accept that we have limitations and that we cannot do it all, and it is okay to humbly ask others for help.

Being humble leaders allows us to see what proud leaders have difficulty seeing—the strengths of others. We have to realize that we are not experts in all things and that it is okay to go to our peers and subordinates and even the leaders above us for their help, for their expertise. In fact, asking others for help, in many ways, empowers your followers. You enable them to see their capabilities. You enable them to see that you recognize their strengths and abilities. When you, as the leader, humble yourself, you set your followers on high. When Pope Francis was going around the East Coast of the United States asking laypeople to pray for him, not only was he humbly recognizing his weaknesses and limitations, but he was also recognizing the strengths and the importance of his followers' voices to God. His request for our prayers for him shows us that we are all in this together, as a family of God. It shows us that our prayers are just as important as his and that he too needs us. He humbles himself so as to build us up and empower us.

> *Do you wish to rise? Begin by descending.*
> *You plan a tower that will pierce the clouds?*
> *Lay first the foundation of humility.*
>
> —Saint Augustine

It does make good engineering sense. If you want to build a high-rise tower, begin by descending and dig deeper for a stronger foundation. Humility is a trait that leaders must have at their core. And it starts even before they respond to the call to lead, before they hold leadership positions. "Humility," as C. S. Lewis said, "is not thinking less of yourself; it's thinking of yourself less."

Mother Teresa, one of the most humble world leaders this world has ever known, never wanted to get credit for any of the work she did. She always said that the things she did were God's work and not hers. And if something was attributed to her, she was quick to dismiss it because she did not want people to "think more of her and less of Jesus."

Fundraising

One area of organizational dynamics that business leaders get involved in is garnering support and raising funds. The health of an organization and its ability to be successful in its missions and operations starts with the leader's ability to gather the necessary resources. In the business world, it is requisite for leaders to have a strong mastery of finding and managing resources, including financial capital. Too often, the financial aspect of leadership becomes a deterrent for many potential leaders to step up and lead.

Leadership studies recognize that fundraising is a difficult skill to develop. It is a task that seems to be onerous and unnecessary for many leaders.

For us Christians, this task is not a walk in the park either. We tend to want to separate what is Caesar's and what is God's.[51] For many Christians, money, both the raising of it and the managing of it, can feel like not only a challenging but an unnecessarily Christian and worldly task. But as we know all too well, obtaining

---
[51] See Mark 12:17

resources, including money, is often a necessary task in doing some of God's work on earth. So let us take a look at the saints' wisdom on this topic and see what we can learn from them about raising funds.

"God Has Lots of Money"

One of the greatest fundraising stories is Mother Teresa's. Mother Teresa raised a lot of funds for the poor, the sick, and the needy. She was able to build religious centers, hospitals, and schools, but the most interesting thing is she never did any active fundraising. She never asked for money, not from the Vatican and not from the government. The constitution of the Missionaries of Charity actually forbids them from asking for money. They relied completely on God's providence to give them the necessary resources they needed to do their missionary work. And as we can see in Mother Teresa's many works around the world, God did so abundantly. One of the co-founders of a religious organization that works with the poorest of the poor in New York, Father Benedict Groeschel, would often recount one of his many conversations with Mother Teresa where Mother told him, "Don't worry, God has lots of money."[52] Mother Teresa had a lot of faith in God's providence, and money did find its way to fund the Missionaries' seven hundred religious centers in over one hundred and thirty countries.

Those leaders involved in fundraising would probably attest to the fact that fundraising is a lot more than just tactics and techniques. Sometimes the raising of funds does not even have to happen deliberately. Sometimes it just happens. Donors and supporters will come when they recognize the trustworthiness

---

[52] Groeschel, Benedict, *Travelers Along the Way: The Men and Women Who Shaped My Life* (Cincinnati, OH: Servant Books, 2010).

of the cause that is driving the mission and the authenticity of the leader and the members. It is human nature to help others in need, but the inclination to help is even greater when the organization and the leaders of the organization are genuine and trustworthy. In general, people want to know exactly what is being done with their donations and contributions. They want to see the link between the cause that they are supporting and the actual outcomes. Mother Teresa's genuine acts, her hands-on approach to her labor of love, demonstrated to the donors and supporters that the work she did went directly to helping the poor, the abandoned, and the dying. And she was always looking for ways to continually serve them. She believed that her work would eventually reach all who needed her care.

And as a result of her genuine acts and her heartfelt vision, money kept pouring in. She made sure that it never went to her or the missionaries but directly to the poor people she served.

When Pope Paul VI visited India, he tried to give Mother Teresa the white limousine that he was riding in as a gift. Mother Teresa never even pictured how luxurious it would be for her to ride in it and so, instead, she raffled the car and used the $100,000 proceeds to start the building of a leper colony.

When she won the Noble Peace Prize in 1979, she refused to attend the dinner banquet in Norway honoring her. She asked the organizers of the banquet that the cost of the dinner, which was $7,000 per person, instead be donated to the poor in India. The people of Norway were so moved by her selfless gesture that they donated even more. They responded to Mother Teresa's request by donating the $7,000 as well as holding the banquet to honor her.

And as we can see here in the case of Mother Teresa, humility and authenticity raise funds.

Capital is Raised by Prayer

In 1933, the Catholic Worker Movement, an organization founded by Dorothy Day and Peter Maurin, also had to rely on divine providence for funds to get their mission going. When Peter and Dorothy were discussing the launch of the newspaper *Catholic Worker*, Dorothy asked the practical question of where they were going to get the money. Peter's response was,

"In the history of the saints, capital was raised by prayer. God sends you what you need when you need it. You will be able to pay for the printer. Just read the lives of the saints."[53] And indeed, the *Catholic Worker* newspaper launched its first issue on May 1, 1933 with twenty-five hundred copies, each copy selling for one penny. Today, eighty-plus years later, it still is published seven times a year.

During the Great Depression in the 1930s, Father Solanus Casey (1870–1957), a Capuchin friar, ran the Soup Kitchen in Detroit with such genuine care for the needy. He had such a reputation for his simple but authentic service to the poor and the hungry that money from various donors just continued trickling in, even despite the devastating economic conditions at that time. The homeless and the poor would knock on the monastery's door, begging for food. Father Solanus simply said to the friars, "They are hungry; let's get them some soup and sandwiches." At the height of the Great Depression, the line to the Soup Kitchen would sometimes reach up to two thousand people, but amazingly, the more people they had to feed, the more the donations came. Father Solanus lived many decades ago, but that Soup Kitchen he ran during the Great Depression still continues to feed the poor in Detroit today.

In the case of Mother Teresa, Dorothy Day, Saint Francis of

---

[53] Mark and Louise Zwick, *Mercy with Borders: The Catholic Worker and Immigration* (Paulist Press: New York, 2010), p.27.

Assisi, Father Solanus Casey, and other saints who raised funds for their causes, the money came as a result of their mission, their vision, and their authenticity. They articulated their vision and their mission, not by words, but by their actions. They stayed true to their vision and mission. Authenticity was at the very core of their personal character as leaders. They gave of themselves and gave up their own material possessions for the sake of others. Their authenticity radiated out. And when a leader is authentic, the people can detect that, and they get inspired to give them offerings with willing hearts (Exodus 25:2).

The rapid growth of their organizations, the Missionaries of Charity, the Catholic Worker Movement, and the Franciscans, is a testament to how authenticity is key to great leadership. They were leaders who were authentic in their beliefs and in their actions. They stayed true and committed to their calling and to their vision.

> *Let us more and more insist on raising funds of love, of kindness, of understanding, of peace. Money will come if we seek first the Kingdom of God—the rest will be given.*
>
> —Mother Teresa

Authentic Leaders

In raising funds, in gathering support, and in building cooperation, it is important for leaders to stay authentic and true to their mission, their vision, and their being. Authenticity is key to effective leadership. In the organizational sciences, groups that are led by authentic leaders tend to have a more positive following. A more positive following leads to positive organizational outcomes.

Lessons in Leadership from the Saints

In our current business atmosphere, especially in light of all the leadership failures and scandals, it seems very hard to find leaders we can trust. We have seen too many leaders, CEOs, sports organizations leaders, government and military leaders, and even church leaders disappoint and fail us. Some failed by misdirection, some failed by scandals, some failed by inauthentic actions. Just think back to the scandalous late 1980s and early 1990s when a whole litany of Christian leaders failed due to moral issues. There was a disconnect between their talk and their walk. What they were preaching and how they were actually behaving did not match, and it made many people very reluctant to trust that kind of supposedly Christian leadership.

Leaders tend to always be in the spotlight, and if there are challenges, leaders are always the first ones to step forward. We can sometimes be too critical of our leaders because we expect so much from them. Unfortunately, many of us have had our share of failed leadership, and so there seems to be a widening gap between the very high standards that we expect from our leaders and how we actually perceive them. Some studies suggest that typical leaders are more often than not perceived to be less honest, less ethical, and less authentic than the average person.

Leaders are smart. But too often, being smart is the one main category we judge them on when we first assign them. We tend to assign individuals to leadership positions who show this trait. However, cognitive intelligence is just one aspect of smart and effective leadership; emotional intelligence and spiritual intelligence are just as important—sometimes even more important. Don't forget that some of the world's most infamous dictators exhibited higher than average cognitive intelligence. Sometimes, smart leaders can be crafty and use their intellect to figure out ways to manipulate their followers and pretend to be someone they are not.

However, no matter how clever they are at pretending, hiding their true self is not easy. Inauthentic traits, especially, are not easy to hide because they will eventually come out. People are always trying to figure out whether they should place their trust in who they are following or not. Inauthentic traits will inevitably find their way to the surface and reveal themselves. Leaders who try to hide their true thoughts, beliefs, and values can only do that for so long because people will figure out their leaders. People have keen eyes for spotting authenticity; they can recognize it, and they can be moved by it because finding an authentic person is like finding a gem. Take, for example, the story of Thomas Malcolm Muggeridge when he spotted the authenticity of Mother Teresa.

Before visiting Mother Teresa in Calcutta for an assigned interview, Thomas Malcolm Muggeridge was an outspoken agnostic with an atheistic leaning. He was a British journalist and a professional cynic known for his very fierce opinions. He would be the last person to come to mind who would have an appreciation for someone like Mother Teresa. Muggeridge was such an unusual resource for catapulting a humble religious nun to international popularity, but he is indeed credited for bringing Mother Teresa to the attention of the world.

It must have been divine providence because it was not his choice to go to Calcutta and interview Mother Teresa. His editor simply did not have any other journalist available for the assignment, and Muggeridge, who was a very unlikely choice for that interview assignment with this simple, humble, and devoted Catholic nun in a far corner of the world, happened to be the only one available at the time.

So off he went to Calcutta to interview Mother Teresa to learn more about her young religious order. Known for his spunk, his cynicism, and his critical nature, Muggeridge must have been prepared to do what he was known to do and that was to question and pick apart Mother Teresa's motivations and beliefs. But little did he know that this moment he had with this humble little nun would have an unexpectedly profound and life-changing impact on him. After he personally met Mother Teresa and witnessed the things that she was doing in India—how she was living, how she was giving all that she had to serve the poor, and how she was genuinely dedicated to doing the work of God, day in and day out—Muggeridge would eventually discover that he had a profound appreciation for such acts. After that interview with Mother Teresa, he was so moved that he wanted to share her story with the world. He would later produce the popular documentary on Mother Teresa called *Something Beautiful for God*. Mother Teresa and her genuine deeds had such an influence on him that he would eventually convert to Catholicism. At the age of seventy-nine, after being an agnostic his entire life, he was baptized into the Catholic Church and eventually become a strong voice for the faith.

Muggeridge was drawn to Mother Teresa's authentic life and leadership. She did all that work never seeking out recognition or fame or money. She had a comfortable life, but she gave up the luxuries that she could have had, only to live with the poor. She worked tirelessly to serve the poor and to show each one of them that they are loved by God. She genuinely lived out her faith, and her entire life and being were devoted to Christ and the poor. Her whole being was a true testimony to God's love here on earth. Muggeridge, who had been a skeptic of humanity's good deeds, saw in Mother Teresa that true authenticity, and that caused him to turn his heart and mind around. Soon after he met Mother Teresa, he went from being an agnostic to a believer. He was so inspired that he shared that gem he just discovered in Calcutta with the rest of the world. The people who learned about Mother Teresa through Muggeridge also spotted her authenticity and her genuine love for God. It is the kind of authenticity that just flows like a river and spreads throughout the landscape, giving life to things along its path. There is something about authenticity that is pure, refreshing, and cleansing. And there is also something about inauthenticity that just does not feel right.

In a 2015 *American Psychological Science* article, researchers

Francesca Gino, Maryam Kouchaki, and Adam Galinsky found that inauthenticity is tied to feelings of impurity and a less moral state.[54] There is a connection between authenticity and positive consequences, and between inauthenticity and negative consequences. Not being true to ourselves can lead to psychological and moral distress. And for followers, there is something naturally appealing about a leaders' authenticity that draws us to follow them. Inauthenticity, on the other hand, pushes people away. We stay away from those leaders as we don't know where they will lead us.

Authentic leadership is a relatively new theory in the management sciences that is gaining popularity, especially in light of the litany of leadership scandals in recent years, but authenticity is not a new virtue at all. From the ancient Greek philosophers to the Enlightenment thinkers, authenticity had always been considered one of the core cardinal human virtues. William Shakespeare wrote in Hamlet, as Polonius's words of wisdom: "To thine own self be true"—a line that is often cited when someone is making a commitment to be true and authentic.

Psychologists Carl Rogers and Abraham Maslow laid the foundation for some of the thinking and discussions that we now have about authentic leadership. Self-actualization, the theory that Maslow had popularized, is a key process for having individuals get in-tune with themselves, and, when doing so, these individuals gain a better understanding of their true, authentic selves. According to Maslow, self-actualizing individuals have strong moral/ethical standards. The more we know ourselves, the more we know our capabilities and our potential as well as our weaknesses and limitations. Self-actualizing individuals have a more accurate picture of who they are, their potential, and their

---

[54] Gino, F., Kouchaki, M., & Galinsky, A.D., *The Moral Virtue of Authenticity: How Inauthenticity Produces Feelings of Immorality and Impurity.* Psychological Science, 2015, Vol.26(7) 983–996.

purpose. Self-actualized individuals maximize their potential and are being the best that they can be. They are aware of their own true self, their strengths, as well as their weaknesses. And as leaders, we need to have self-awareness. We will not be able to lead others if we cannot lead ourselves. We are the leaders of our own lives. As leaders, let us heed Plato's advice to "know thyself."

> *It is the greatest of all lessons to know oneself. For if one knows oneself one will know God, and knowing God, that person will be made like God.*
>
> *—Clement of Alexandria*

In leadership scholarship, authenticity has been a very popular topic, especially in recent literature, but despite the many ways scholars have talked about it, the concept of authentic leadership is not easy to define. But most people can recognize what authentic leadership looks like and tell it apart from plastic, inauthentic leadership. They can gauge leaders and determine when to follow or not to follow. They can detect the consistency or inconsistency between words and deeds. Followers just have that gut feeling and can sense that.

> *Let us now come to the time of trial—for we can only test ourselves by watching our actions narrowly, and we shall soon detect signs of deception.*
>
> *—Saint Teresa of Avila.*

When Muggeridge met Mother Teresa, he knew there was something special and genuine about her that was worthy of sharing with others. He knew that Mother Teresa was on a path to something good and that it was a path that he knew he wanted to follow. And so in a way, he did follow that path. He converted to Catholicism and became an outspoken voice for the faith. And because of him, the world got to know Mother Teresa and the many wonderful things she did. He introduced Mother Teresa to the world. He produced the documentary film *Something Beautiful for God* and the book with the same title, which are both about Mother Teresa and the work that she was doing in India. Many of us got to know the authenticity of Mother Teresa as well as the path that she was on because of Muggeridge. And thanks to him, many of us now have a template for humble and servant leadership to follow. The whole world got to know what it is like to serve God authentically and with humility. And with Muggeridge's initial introduction of Mother Teresa to the world, other wonderful works followed to give us more details about Mother Teresa. We now have details of the path she took—that path that leads up to doing God's work, to holiness, and to closeness with God—a path laid out for us to follow.

Pope Francis is another leadership figure that embodies authenticity. His simple and humble ways are very similar to Mother Teresa's ways, perhaps because they are getting their marching orders from the same loving God. His actions are authentic, and people can detect that and so they follow him and flock around him. His words are consistent with his deeds. He not only preaches evangelical poverty, but he tries to live it. His black shoes, his bus trips, and his very modest style all speak volumes about him and his principles. So when he goes preaching about the poor, people listen. They listen to his words of wisdom. They draw inspiration from him. People place their trust in his leadership because they know that he is authentic. His flock allows him to shepherd them because they know he is genuinely leading them closer to God.

Leadership Based on Values

Values are the guiding principle in our lives—our own personal lives, our organizations, and our society. Leadership begins with one's values. The choices and decisions we will make in life are going to be consistent with the values we hold. Leading successfully and effectively is impossible without values informing our mission, our vision, and why we do what we do.

Some examples of values that drive leaders and organizations are:

Respect
Courage
Authenticity
Humility
Service
Integrity
Wisdom
Compassion
Trust
Commitment
Sacrifice

In the gospel, Jesus Christ spoke of values such as joy, peace, justice, hope, and love. As followers of Christ, we are called to uphold these same values. We need to understand these values and their meaning in our lives for they will guide our actions toward our goals, particularly our heavenly goals.

As leaders, it is even more important to have our values clarified and defined. Followers expect their leaders to guide them toward the shared vision and toward achieving the common goal. The core values, the activities, and the mission of the organization will likely reflect the values of its leader. That means the followers, the members of the organization, will carry with them personal values that align with the values not only of the organization but also of their leaders. Values stem from the leaders and flows throughout the organization. Values build our bonds and solidifies our interdependence with one another. Individuals who are disconnected from the values of the leader and the organization are not going to be effective contributors. But individuals who are strongly connected to the values of the organization, individuals who have internalized those values and adopted them as their own, will be very effective contributors to the accomplishment of the mission.

Mission-Driven

> *Therefore, go and make disciples of all nations, baptizing them in the name of the Father and of the Son and of the Holy Spirit, and teaching them to obey everything I have commanded you. And surely I am with you always, to the very end of the age.*
>
> *—Matthew 28:19–20*

One central aspect of leadership as identified by many leadership studies, especially in recent times, is being mission-driven. And if it is an indication of the times, the generations that are now coming in droves into the workplace do expect to have a connection to the mission of the organization. According to a report by Deloitte, "The Millennial Survey 2014: Big Demands and High Expectations," 70 percent of millennials expect their organizations to focus on being mission-driven.[55] They look for such organizations because they know that they want to do something that they can contribute to, something that they can have a connection with. Mission-driven workplaces attract innovators and high-performers.

At the heart of any organization is the mission. In the case of the saints, they knew what their missions were. They were not walking around aimlessly in life; they did not fight like a boxer beating the air (1 Corinthians 9:26). They knew their purpose in life; they knew what God had called them to do. The word *mission* in Latin means "to send." The saints, through their prayerful discernment, came to know what God sent them to do. They clearly understood their calling, and they devoted themselves to it.

Leaders must know clearly what their mission is and that they must also know how to align their actions to the mission. And as leaders, they need to make sure there is alignment between the mission and their actions. They also need to make sure there is alignment between the actions of their followers and the mission as well. They need to know how to coordinate their followers' actions around the mission.

> *May it please the supreme and divine Goodness to give us all abundant grace ever to know His most holy will and perfectly to fulfill it.*
>
> —*Saint Ignatius of Loyola*

Saint Francis Xavier had plans to pursue the intellectual life as an academic scholar. Even his mentor and leader, Saint Ignatius, had plans to deploy him as a scholar for their new religious order. But as it turned out, he found that God had other plans for him.

---

[55] Deloitte, "The Millennial Survey 2014: Big Demands and High Expectations." Accessed from www.deloitte.com on June 10, 2016.

Ignatius did not want to send Francis Xavier too far, but during such busy times of their growth, he really did not have any choice but to send him to Asia, where his services were needed by the Church. And so Francis Xavier graciously accepted God's mission for him, and off he went to Asia. There, he preached the Good News tirelessly, and he fulfilled his mission all the way to his dying days. His followers and the locals he educated knew and understood his mission. His followers saw the fire in his eyes. They saw his conviction, his devotion, and his dedication to the mission, and so they carried it out and kept the fire that Francis Xavier ignited burning. He was able to coordinate the actions of his followers around the mission and so, even today, hundreds of years later, many of the missions Francis Xavier started and established still continue to stand and even flourish.

Vision with Purpose

The greatest challenge of the day is: how to bring about a revolution of the heart, a revolution which has to start with each one of us.

—Dorothy Day

Many of the great feats in our world started with a vision. Mankind was able to go to the moon because of John F. Kennedy's vision. Apple's founder Steve Jobs had a vision. Tesla's CEO Elon Musk had a vision. Albert Einstein, Thomas Edison, and other great figures of history each had a vision that propelled them to do great things. Mankind has made so much progress over time because of visionary leaders, and humanity owes them a great deal.

Many of the saints were able to accomplish their calling because they had vision. Mother Teresa had a vision so that the impoverished and the sick would not have to die alone. Dorothy Day, a convert to Catholicism and founder of the Catholic Worker Movement, had a vision of equality and justice, and she worked tirelessly so that she could do her part to elevate the poor working-class from poverty. She established hospitality houses for the poor, which now number over a hundred across the country. These leaders had a vision, and not necessarily in the mystical sense as Saint Joan of Arc experienced or what Saint Paul experienced in his journey to Damascus. It is the kind of vision that visionary leaders see. It is the kind of vision where they can see with their discerning mind's eyes what God is calling them to do. Their vision comes from God, and they become stewards of those visions, and they carry them out and execute them. Visionary leaders have an extraordinary vision of a better world, a better future, and a world where there is more good than evil. They are champions of change. They envision that they can change the world, and their very vision starts with them. They start the change they envisioned by carrying out the work themselves, and they communicate their vision clearly to others by their exemplary genuine actions.

Saint Dominic de Guzman of Spain, a contemporary of Saint Francis of Assisi, had a charismatic vision of communities of committed men and women living the apostolic life. During the time of Dominic, many parish priests and monks were living lavish and opulent lifestyles, unable to respond to the spiritual needs of the people. The clergy had distanced themselves from the values of the gospel, and so the people, in turn, started to distance themselves from the church. Dominic realized there was a need for change in the Church, and so he, with prayer and discernment, decided to do something about it. With the vision he had, he then went out to seek reform in hopes of bringing people back to the Church and getting them to trust the priests again. He started to teach priests how to preach in a simple and humble manner. He founded the Order of Preachers, one of the largest religious organizations still going strong today. This religious order is more recognizable today as the Dominicans. The three formal vows that Dominican friars make—obedience, poverty, and chastity—are vows that stand to counter the misguided lifestyles of the clergy during Dominic's time. These vows not only appealed to the hearts and minds of the laity, but they also allow the friars to live unfettered in imitation of Jesus Christ.

Having a vision is one thing, but understanding the purpose of the vision is another thing. The saints not only had a vision, but they also understood their purpose. Consider the parable of the three bricklayers. There are many different variations in the way this parable has been told, but I particularly like Angela Duckworth's rendition in her book *Grit*.[56] In her rendition, there were three bricklayers, and each one of them was asked what they were doing.

The first bricklayer replied, "I am laying bricks."

The second bricklayer said, "I am building a church."

The third bricklayer said, "I am building the house of God."

In other words, the first bricklayer has a job; the second has a career, and the third has a calling or a vocation.

This parable, which is usually used to illustrate purpose-driven vocations, is an enlightening parable that illustrates the purpose that the saints found in their calling. The saints knew and understood their purpose, and it was not just to either lay down bricks in order to have a building or to build a church in order for people to have a structure to pray in. They treated their response

---

[56] Angela Duckworth, *Grit: The Power of Passion and Perseverance* (New York, NY: Simon & Schuster, 2016), p.149.

to their calling not as a job or as a career. They knew the ultimate purpose of what they were called to do, and that is to serve God. They had a vocation. The word *vocation* comes from the Latin root word *vocare*, which means "to call." The saints, with their hearts and ears open, heard the call of God summoning them to what they needed to do. And their response became their vocation and their purpose in life.

> *Be who God meant you to be and you will set the world on fire.*
>
> —Saint Catherine of Siena

When Saint Francis of Assisi realized that his calling was a lot more than just rebuilding the physical structure of San Damiano, he started to rebuild the spiritual Church of God. He aligned everything that he did in his life to operationalize that calling. He saw a vision of what Christ was calling him to do. His everyday actions and his interactions with everyone around him were all aligned to that vision.

Saint Francis had a vision to rebuild the church as God had called him to do and so he did. He rebuilt the church both physically and spiritually. And thanks to his vision, we now have a leader in Pope Francis who draws inspiration from that same vision. If you want to get a glimpse of what that vision looks like in action, just follow the works of our dear Pope Francis. He is, in so many ways, rebuilding the spiritual Church of God.

Ability to Empower

Having a vision is just one step, but, nonetheless, a fundamental one in leadership success. Leadership starts with a vision, but leaders must be able to translate that vision into reality. A leader's vision is no good if it merely stays a vision. A vision must be followed by communication and empowerment. Ignatius shared his vision with his very good friends, Francis Xavier and Peter Faber, and that vision empowered them to go out on their own, even to uncharted territories, so that they could share that same vision with the rest of the world. Francis Xavier clearly understood Ignatius's vision as well as the practice of the *Spiritual Exercises* that Ignatius developed. He shared the same vision. Francis Xavier, in turn, communicated that vision to his followers and mentees in Asia. He empowered his own followers, who would become Jesuits, to carry out the vision of the Society of Jesus. And so not only did the new Jesuits help spread the vision of Francis Xavier and Ignatius, but they also continued it for them. That same vision has been going strong from one generation to the next, even unto today. Pope Francis, our Church leader today, is a Jesuit whose leadership vision is one that we can trace all the way back to the 1500s, all the way back to its founder, Saint Ignatius.

This succession of Jesuit leaders is an illustration of what great leadership is about. As leadership expert, Tom Peters said, "True leaders don't create more followers; they create more leaders." Saint Ignatius created a great leader in Saint Francis Xavier by trusting in him, by inspiring him, and by empowering him.

In today's scientific studies, research shows that empowered teams are more productive and more proactive than teams that are less empowered.[57] Gone are the days of leaders who overpower.

---

[57] See Bradley Kirkman & Benson Rosen, "Beyond Self-Management: Antecedents and Consequences of Team Empowerment," *Journal of Academy of Management*, Vol.42, No.1 (February 1, 1999).

Instead, the time is now ripe for leaders who empower. In today's knowledge economy, there is an emphasis on placing a high value on the skills, knowledge, and talent that every individual brings to the table. Empowerment, and not coercion or dominance, is the key to unlocking their potential to contribute to the mission.

Empowering others is an important characteristic of leadership, and it is a lot more than just delegating or enabling followers to carry out a task. Empowerment is treating the followers as capable individuals and giving them a sense of ownership of the task and entrusting them to make good decisions on their own. According to author, speaker, and one of the leading authorities on leadership, Mark Sanborn, "True leadership is defined as the invitation to greatness extended to others." Empowering others is helping them reach deep within themselves and to draw out their maximum potential to do great things. Saint Ignatius, as the superior general of his religious order, drew the best out of Saint Francis Xavier and Peter Faber and empowered them to venture out to far distant lands to win people for the greater glory of God. As the Jesuits say, *"Ad Majorem Dei Gloriam!"* Francis Xavier and Peter Faber carried out their assignments as their very own mission in life. They understood their roles, the tasks ahead, and they knew what they had to do to get the job done. Saint Francis Xavier, while in Asia, accepted that going out as a missionary was his own calling even though he had other plans early on in his life. He was planning to pursue the university life, but when Saint Ignatius helped him realize his calling, he took it as his own. He accepted his calling as God's plan for him, and he became great at it. Thanks to the empowering leadership of Saint Ignatius and to the missionary zeal of Saint Francis Xavier, we are now the beneficiaries of having him and Saint Therese of Lisieux as the patron saints of missionaries, who have laid out the foundation and the template for us for doing God's work with other cultures.

In the Bible, we see this example of empowerment play out between Saint Paul and the younger Timothy. In the letters of

Saint Paul to Timothy are words of empowerment from a mentor to a mentee. After mentoring Timothy for many years, Saint Paul sensed that it was time for him to go soon and that he was ready to pass on the torch. Saint Paul empowered Timothy to carry the mission forward, to continue his preaching ministry for he would one day pass the same torch on to others in future generations who would be qualified and reliable to teach and defend the gospel (2 Timothy 2:2).

In the organizational settings that we have today, empowering others is an important aspect of leadership. Leaders today recognize that their leadership is most effective when they empower others to lead. And the younger generations respond better when they are empowered. Empowerment means a lot in today's culture, both as either a recipient or a giver, or as a leader or a follower. According to a 2015 survey by WorkPlaceTrends.com and Virtuli, millennials do not care much for legacy and that they would rather choose to empower others than to get recognized. In a well-informed society that we now live in, empowering others is the way to lead and be led. This will probably be the norm that the younger generations get used to. Millennials today are growing up differently than the previous generations. They are growing up in a social culture that promotes a social environment that is more nurturing. There's more emphasis on cooperative learning and on empowering rather than overpowering. Gone are the days of leadership when leaders say, "Do as I say." Followers are more interested in leadership that silently speaks, "Do as I do." Verbally commanding their followers to follow is often ineffective, so leaders must recognize that it is better to lead by empowering and inspiring. Leaders must be able to place their trust in their followers. They must be able to have confidence in their followers to have their own creative thinking, decision-making, and actions. Leaders must enable and empower their followers to draw out their maximum potential. They must focus on advancing not themselves but their followers and making them great.

Kapwa Tao

In the Filipino culture, the culture of my upbringing, there is a core value called *kapwa*, and it is a concept of personhood that differentiates the Filipino culture from other cultures. The concept of *kapwa* is "at the core of Filipino social psychology and at the heart of the structure of Filipino values."[58] *Kapwa* is a uniquely Filipino concept and a word that is not easy and straightforward to translate. In English, perhaps the literal translation that reflects this concept best is "shared togetherness." We can even say that it can be translated as "shared inner self" as proposed by Virgilio Enriquez, a Filipino psychologist hailed as the father of modern Filipino psychology. *Kapwa* shows the ethos of how we ought to care for one another and that we share our inner self with others. *Kapwa* speaks of that one unifying essence that shows that we are on this journey to get closer to God together. In the Catechism of the Catholic Church, we are called to treat others as another self,[59] with respect and dignity. As leaders, we need to realize our shared togetherness and to see the other as another human being, a child of God created in the Divine image. We need to see this special bond that we have with one another.

---

[58] Pe-Pua, R. & Protacio-Marcelino, E., "Sikolohiyang Pilipino (Filipino Psychology): A Legacy of Virgilio G. Enriquez." *Asian Journal of Social Psychology* (2000)3:49–71

[59] Catholic Church, 1931 in Catechism of the Catholic Church. 2nd ed. Vatican: Libreria Editrice Vaticana, 2000.

BJ Gonzalvo, Ph.D.

Physical Fitness

One overlooked element of leadership is physical fitness. According to a 2013 *Wall Street Journal* article,[60] being physically fit is a very important leadership characteristic. It is important for leaders to be in excellent shape, to prepare physically, mentally, and emotionally for the stressful business challenges that they have to face on a daily basis. Leaders must recognize the connection between the body and the mind, between being in good physical shape and being mentally and emotionally fit.

When we get overwhelmed by all the different priorities we have in life, we tend to end up neglecting our own physical health, including our physical fitness. We can learn from Father Solanus Casey (1850-1957), an American Capuchin friar and a recent candidate for beatification, because he seemed to have valued not only the spiritual virtues but the virtue of being physically fit. He seemed to have put spirituality and physical fitness together when so many others dichotomized them. He was ordained a priest, but he was also a doorkeeper and a porter for his religious order. As a porter, he always had to be ready and available for the needs and demands of the other friars. And he took this porter role seriously, and he practiced it wholeheartedly. He worked in the soup kitchen a lot, particularly during the height of the Great Depression. The friary where he worked stayed busy during this time, and a lot of families in need came for food. He had to be fit to endure all the physical labor and service he had to fulfill. Some people saw him "jogging" around the friary to stay in shape and keep up with the physical demands of his job. And this was even before the idea of jogging became popular and cool. He would run up and down the stairs as part of his daily routine. He incorporated recreation in his daily activities, and he would join the younger friars in

---

[60] Kwoh, L. "Want to be a CEO? What's Your BMI?" (January 16, 2013). *Wall Street Journal*.

playing team sports, such as volleyball and tennis, to stay in good physical shape. Even going into his late seventies, he remained in good physical shape and still able to physically attend to the needs of the visitors that came to the friary. His commitment to physical fitness was key to his service.

We now have extensive research backing up various claims, such as that staying physically fit makes us more productive, it helps build stamina and endurance, it helps us stay alert, it wards off diseases, and it helps us manage stress. As leaders, how can we be the source of energy when we ourselves lack energy? But we have to keep in mind that we must not treat physical fitness as an end in itself. Rather, we should remember that it is a means to an end. We have to keep in mind what the end goal is, and that is to serve God and His people. Physical fitness is just one part of the whole, and it must not be separated from the spiritual dimensions because we need the whole person to mobilize all his or her available energies in order to fulfill his or her vocation and for the good of others.

Father Solanus Casey tried to stay in good shape, not for himself but so that he could continue to serve the people of God. He took care of his own physical body so that he could perform the tasks assigned to him. As servants of God today, especially given what now know about the benefits of exercise and physical fitness, we have to take care of our bodies—our tools for doing God's work on earth. We need to respect our bodies and realize that our bodies are a temple of God, with the spirit of God living in us (1 Corinthians 3:16). When we are tired, it is important that we get some rest to relieve stress and to revitalize so that we can perform our Christian duties to the best of our abilities and endure as we run the race (Hebrew 12:1). In the latest research in psychology, we see it is important to rest the brain because the brain allows us to continuously restore and sustain our overall well-being. Leaders are expected to be able to perform their best and carry not only themselves but their followers as well. We have to maintain the alignment between our mental well-being and physical well-being if we want to truly maximize our abilities. Research has found that there is a direct correlation between the maintenance of our well-being and the increased incidence of health and safety problems.[61]

In the New Testament, as the apostles returned from the work that they were sent out to do, they came back tired and had not had a chance to eat. Jesus said to them, "Come with me by yourselves to a quiet place and get some rest" (Mark 6:31). Doing the work of the Lord is not easy and can take a physical toll. We have to take care and prepare so that we can endure and do more, so that we can help the weak, and so that we can give more (Acts 20:35). As leaders, others will be relying on us and our abilities to work and make decisions. They will be following our example and drawing strength from us. May we draw strength from God and may we be able to continually lead His people to Him.

> *Let us go forward in peace, our eyes upon heaven, the only goal of our labors.*
>
> *—Saint Therese of Lisieux*

Like an Athlete

Athletes nowadays fully maximize the latest information about exercise so that they can perform above and beyond their capabilities. And we can learn a lot from athletes because doing God's work demands our very best. Doing God's work requires the same kind of dedication that athletes practice to make sure their

---

[61] Sluiter, J.K., *The Influence of Work Characteristics on the Need for Recovery and Experienced Health: A Study on Coach Drivers.* Journal of Ergonomics, 42 (1999) Issue 4.

bodies can meet the challenges of their sport. We also have to give it our all as we do God's work and as we serve others.

Athletes are excellent examples of not only physical fitness but also of persistence, perseverance, and grit. Great elite athletes have these traits. They know how to overcome their limitations and adversities. In sports, we often hear players from the losing side say that they will come back stronger and better. Athletes with good leadership skills who get defeated will figure out a way to bounce back. They do not dwell on the past nor do they get emotionally bogged down by failure. If they do, it can have damaging and contagious effects on them, and they could potentially end up dragging their team down with them. Great leader athletes will accept the defeat and move on to the next challenge, train harder, carry their team on their backs, and work to bounce back. They do not give up easily. They are gritty and they have confidence and trust in their abilities that they can overcome setbacks and achieve victory. They have what is called in psychology "positive explanatory style." Individuals with positive explanatory style tend to have an optimistic outlook on life versus a negative outlook. They do not fall into despair or become paralyzed by their lack of confidence. Instead, they try to figure out why they lost and how to recover and come back stronger. They try to identify the weaknesses and the problems that they need to work on. Once they identify the weaknesses, they accept it and they put in the work to get better and improve their game.

We admire those athletes who, despite a loss, are quick to acknowledge what they did wrong and how they plan to make corrections and improvements in their game to get ready for the next match or the next opportunity to play a better game. We like their stories. We like to watch them overcome and rise up to the challenge. We draw inspiration from people like them.

That same trait of perseverance and grit can also be found in the saints. Saints are probably not the first to come to mind when you think of athleticism these days but the saints do have some of the qualities that great athletes possess to overcome challenges and attain victory. Think of Saint Joan of Arc, Saint Ignatius of Loyola, Saint Francis Xavier, Saint Therese of Lisieux, and countless others. It was not necessarily their physical athleticism because some of them actually were far from the way we imagine physical athleticism these days. Saint Ignatius had a deformity in his leg. Saint Giles, the patron saint of cripples, was himself crippled. Saint Therese of Lisieux had poor physical health. Blessed Margaret of Castello was born blind, with severe curvature of the spine, and was a dwarf. And yet, their physical limitations did not hinder them from doing great things for God. Despite the broken leg and the heavy limp, Saint Ignatius would later found one of the biggest religious orders in the world today. Despite being crippled after having been struck by an arrow, Saint Giles founded a monastery. Despite birth defects like being blind and a dwarf, and despite having been abandoned as a child, Blessed Margaret of Castello was able to find her purpose in life and successfully run a school for her town.

The Saints might not be the typical athletes that we are accustomed to these days, but they have certainly endured the race, persevered through some of the most arduous hardships, and bounced back from some of the most debilitating setbacks. To me, they are the true champions, well-deserving of the heavenly rewards that they all relish right now. Their strong mental and spiritual abilities pushed them beyond their limits. Just like some of the athletes we admire today, the saints were always working on their game and looking for improvements in their spiritual life.

The saints have confidence not necessarily in themselves but in God's grace. The saints recognized their strengths and abilities from God, honed them, and used them to the best of their abilities to serve God and to give back. They also recognized their weaknesses, and they worked on them to make improvements. Many of them stumbled and fell, but it was during those difficult times that they realized how great and how constant God's love is. They bounced back, and they allowed God's love to carry them to persevere and endure all the way to the end.

> *Therefore, since we are surrounded by so great a cloud of witnesses, let us throw off everything that hinders and the sin that so easily entangles. And let us run with perseverance the race that is marked out for us.*
>
> *—Hebrews 12:1*

Spiritual Fitness

The saints have another dimension to their leadership that enables them to carry out their day-to-day mission. It is also a weighty and important dimension for leaders to have, especially in today's world. That leadership dimension is spiritual fitness. Leaders must recognize the importance of being spiritually fit to be able to carry out their missions and to persevere and endure challenges when doing God's work. They know where to draw their strength from, and that is from God, through prayer. They train and build spiritual muscles by praying and having deep conversations with God.

My spiritual director back when I had just reverted back to the Catholic faith, Father Dan, would wake up way before sunrise so that he could prepare for the day that lay ahead for a very busy parish priest. He said that the busier his day was, the longer he would pray. What he said made me think. This was when I realized that gaining extra energy does not necessarily come from getting that extra hour of sleep. It comes from prayer. God is the true and eternal source of our strength. And Father Dan was right; the more tasks we have ahead, the more we should pray.

> *Half-an-hour's meditation each day is essential, except when you are busy. Then a full hour is needed.*
>
> —*Saint Francis De Sales*

I even started to notice it in the stories of the lives of the saints. The busier they got and the more difficult the tasks ahead were, the more they prayed. Saint Joan of Arc drew her strength from God through prayer. When she was wounded in battle, struck by an arrow above her breast, she removed the arrow with her bare hands, went away to a secluded place to pray, came right back to her troops, and led them to victory.

When Saint Francis Xavier failed in Japan the first time he went there, he withdrew and left. But as he was leaving on a boat, he prayed, and through prayer and discernment, he was able to draw wisdom and strength to carry on. He turned the boat around and headed back to Japan, invigorated with a new strategy. He changed his clothing and his mannerisms. He adapted to the cultural practices and learned the language. He was eventually able to get an audience with the emperor and reach out to the wider local population.

> *It is not the actual physical exertion that counts towards one's progress ... but by the spirit of faith with which it is undertaken.*
>
> —*Saint Francis Xavier*

Persistence, Perseverance, and Grit

Challenges and difficulties are likely to arise. And leaders are aware of these facts of life. But what separates leaders from the rest is their determination to reach their goals and succeed in their mission. They always find a way to get through. Successful leadership must always be looking for ways to overcome challenges and difficulties. Successful leadership has persistence and grit.

Persistence is a key attribute of leadership success. As many of us know, doing the work of the Lord is not always easy. To be able to carry out our mission does require persistence. Christopher Peterson and Martin Seligman defined persistence as "voluntary continuation of a goal-oriented action in spite of obstacles, difficulties, or discouragement."[62] There will be obstacles and difficulties. There will be times when we will be discouraged. But leaders press on. They will find a way to continue to reach their goals.

Leaders are gritty. We are all aware how important intelligence and talent are in achieving success in any professional domain, but grit seems to be the one personality trait that exceptional individuals have to take it all the way to achieving greatness. Grit is what pushes these individuals above and beyond the limitations and even into the impossible.

Grit is defined as perseverance and passion for a long-term goal. Many of the saints we know are paragons of grit. Think about Saint Ignatius after getting his legs hit by a cannonball that rendered him unable to walk normally again and unable to attain the military glory that he had been pursuing his whole life. In fact, his injuries were so bad that the doctors told him to prepare for death. He suffered a setback that he considered a

---

[62] Peterson, C. & Seligman, M. (2004). *Character Strengths and Virtues: A Handbook and Classification*. Oxford University Press.

fate worse than death, and he even contemplated suicide.[63] It is hard to imagine our current state of Catholic spirituality if Saint Ignatius had given up during that time of extraordinary setback. Catholicism would not be the same if he did not have the courage, the perseverance, and the grit to bounce back from this kind of setback. We would not have the beloved *Spiritual Exercises* if he had not persevered. We would not have Jesuits today making a difference in the world. We would not have some of these great Jesuits schools, universities, and other institutions that are now so much an integral part of our society. We owe Saint Ignatius of Loyola for having such grit, for persevering, and for his courage to overcome.

Another example of grit that easily comes to mind is that of Saint Joan of Arc. The heroic story of Joan of Arc is widespread, and it is one that is notable for courage, persistence, perseverance, and grit. Joan of Arc encountered many difficulties along the way that many of us might not be able to endure. It was grit that made her stand up to those challenges and endure them all the way to her last day.

As a young peasant girl from the countryside, she was unknown to everyone. And yet, with her persistence and her focus on her goal, she would figure out a way to get an audience with church leaders, military leaders, and eventually, the king of France. Before her military leadership, she did not know how to fight or ride a horse, but she did all that with valor and grace as she led the French army from one victory to another. When she got seriously wounded in battle, she bounced back and rejoined her troops to keep up their morale and courage. She was eventually captured and handed over to the inquisition for trial as a heretic, charged with immodesty, wearing male clothing, and relying on the divine revelation she had over the authority of the Church.

---

[63] Donnelly, J.P. (2004). *Ignatius of Loyola, Founder of the Jesuits*. Pearson Education.

There were several attempts by her captors to persuade her to recant in order to avoid punishment and the death sentence. But she maintained her authenticity and everything that she stood for, even if it meant her death and getting burnt at the stake. She had a higher goal that she pursued relentlessly and tirelessly. She faced so many obstacles and difficulties, but she was gritty about pursuing that goal.

> *You need to persevere so that when you have done the will of God, you will receive what He has promised.*
>
> *—Hebrews 10:36*

Saint Paul mentioned perseverance many times in his preaching. When I visited Turkey in the late 1990s, I got to stand in one of the cave churches where Saint Paul is believed to have preached. I was in the US military serving on tour in Turkey—the land referred to in biblical times as *Asia Minor*. I consider myself very blessed to have had that opportunity to be there in such a biblical place, retracing the footsteps of Saint Paul the Apostle and getting to experience the lives of the first Christians. I was only stationed in Turkey for several weeks, so on my days off, I would often jump at the opportunity to join a tour of the historical landmarks of the region. And these landmarks were all over the place. I got to visit Tarsus, the birthplace of Saint Paul, and the well where it is believed to be built in his birthplace. But one of the remarkable landmarks that stands out in my memory is the cave church. Our churches today are above ground and very visible but imagine what it was like during the first years of Christianity, a time when Christianity was not accepted and believers were persecuted for their faith. The caves in Turkey served as hiding places and churches for the early Christians. As I stood in that cave church, I couldn't help but imagine Saint Paul preaching in those caves with great courage as he tried to escape the authorities trying to persecute him. Getting caught practicing and preaching Christianity could mean death. He had been imprisoned, flogged severely, exposed to death again and again (see 2 Corinthians 11:23-26), and yet, there he was giving it his all—all for the glory of the kingdom of God. Christianity has come a long way from those days and there are generations upon generations of Christians, including me, who have Saint Paul to thank for enduring and persevering. I stood in that cave church humbled and honored, thinking about what Saint Paul did for us.

Grit is one intangible characteristic that makes many of our great leaders and great saints stand out from the rest of us. In some of the latest research, particularly some of the research done by Angela Duckworth, developer of the grit scale and author of the book *Grit—The Power of Passion and Perseverance*, it is found that grittier individuals are more likely to accomplish things. Grittier individuals are more likely to finish school, may it be a two-year college, a four-year college, or graduate school; grittier individuals are more likely to earn higher GPAs; they are more likely to get through rigorous and selective programs like West Point. Among the cadets at the United States Military Academy West Point, those who scored higher on the grit scale were more likely to get through the rigorous summer training program called Beast Barracks. At the Scripps National Spelling Bee, Duckworth found that grit was a better predictor of advancing to the finals.[64] The Spelling Bee participants were known to have gone through hundreds of solitary deliberate practice per year. These participants devoted at least 10 hours per week practicing! Imagine what these young kids have to give up in order to participate.

Grittier individuals are not necessarily smarter or more

---

[64] Angela Lee Duckworth, T.A. Kirby, E. Tsukuyam, H. Berstein, and K.A. Ericsson, "Deliberate Practice Spells Success: Why Grittier Competitors Truimps at the National Spelling Bee." *Social Psychological and Personality Science, 2(2)* (2011), 174-181.

talented than the rest. What makes them grittier is that they study more, they practice more, and they exercise more. They are more persistent. They have self-discipline. They have set their eyes on the prize, and they are willing to endure and persevere, whatever it takes to finish the race. Despite whatever adversities and struggles get thrown their way, they will choose to overcome.

It takes a lot of grit to get through life and come out at the end as a saint. Saint Joan of Arc, Saint Ignatius, Saint Therese of Lisieux, and many other gritty saints suffered tremendously, and they got through some of the toughest and harshest conditions any human being can face. However, there is one more thing that these gritty saints had to get through it all. There is one special ingredient that makes these saints even grittier than everybody else—that is prayer. They prayed deliberately. Their prayer, their action, and their grit were all for the attainment of that one goal, and that is to do God's will. In the final chapter, we will discuss this factor in greater detail to illustrate the value of prayer in leadership.

> *Prayer is the deliberate and persevering action of the soul. It is true and enduring, full of grace. Prayer fastens the soul to God and makes it one with God's will.*
>
> —Saint Julian of Norwich

Practice and Preparation

Another complementary factor to grit is self-discipline. Musicians and athletes know that in order to be good at what they do, they have to be committed to developing themselves; and they know that becoming good takes discipline. They spend hours practicing their craft and essentially building muscle memory. Steph Curry, one of the best shooters in basketball today, spends countless hours shooting the basketball from virtually every corner of the court. He practices shooting at least a hundred times a day and doing several challenging drills to get ready for the game. Same with one of football's greatest quarterbacks, Peyton Manning. Manning would spend countless hours each week diligently practicing and preparing. He was certainly talented and gifted to be an NFL quarterback but he knew that he still had to work extra hard to accomplish the things he did. In an interview after he announced his retirement from the NFL, he said: "There were other players that were more talented, but there was no one who could out-prepare me."[65]

According to Malcolm Gladwell, author of the book *Outliers*, many of the elite performers have typically practiced their craft for at least ten thousand hours. Gladwell points out that even computer programmers like Bill Gates and Paul Allen had acquired ten thousand hours of practice prior to launching their software in 1975. They practiced their craft deliberately. Greatness comes to these elite performers not because of sheer luck or talent but because they have practiced and prepared.

Living a saintly life as well as being a leader also takes countless hours of practice and preparation. Leaders and saints became who they are because they put in the work and the effort. They practiced holiness deliberately. When it comes to becoming a leader or a saint, it is a lot more than just talent or any natural abilities. And they certainly did not become leaders or saints overnight. Saints and leaders are individuals who, in their response to their calling, have devoted spending countless hours to honing their craft, praying, studying, and pursuing their calling.

---

[65] Seth Walder, "Emotional Peyton Manning Has 'No Regrets' in Announcing Retirement from Broncos and NFL," *New York Daily News,* March 7, 2016.

Part of our daily practice as Christians trying to perfect our craft should include spending the time and effort to recognize what our strengths and weaknesses are. We must be able to identify what those are so that we can practice and develop our strengths, and rectify and strengthen the areas where we are weak. Once we recognize our strengths and weaknesses, and humbly accept them, we can then start working on them, developing them, and cultivating them to achieve perfection.

Self-Reflection Toward Perfection

Like the ancient Greeks said, "Know thyself," Knowing thyself is a key step to becoming a leader and a saint. Saint Teresa of Avila said in her book, *Interior Castle*: "It is no small pity, and should cause us no little shame, that, through our own fault, we do not understand ourselves, or know who we are." Leadership is an ongoing process of self-knowledge and self-discovery. As leaders and as Christians, we have to take the time to examine who we are, remember what we are trying to do, and know what our values are. Knowing thyself is a simple advice for leaders but it is no easy task. Being able to monitor our behaviors, emotions, and reactions requires diligence and effort. What makes it even more challenging is that there is often a disconnect between how we perceive ourselves and how others perceive us. We tend to inflate our self-appraisals. We need to practice and sharpen our metacognition ability.

According to cognitive psychologists, metacognition simply means to think about thinking. Leaders must have this ability to think about their thinking in order to have awareness of their own cognitive process and their assumptions. Having such awareness enables them to control their thinking, emotions, reactions, and strategies. This ability allows us not only to assess ourselves but also to correct ourselves and to bring forth our best selves.

As Catholics, we are blessed to have the Sacrament of Penance for this is our opportunity to examine our conscience. This Sacrament gives us the opportunity to reflect on our deeds and our words. This is our opportunity not just to repent of our sins but also to know ourselves and examine our lives and the areas in our lives that can use improvement as we all strive for perfection. As Jesus told His followers, "Be perfect as God in heaven is perfect" (Matthew 5:48). The examination of conscience and our act of contrition, combined with our humble seeking of God's grace for us to overcome our weaknesses and develop our strengths, are the tools we need as we strive for perfection.

It's just like when we hear some of the elite athletes talk about perfecting their game. When they fail, they don't despair; they accept and acknowledge their failures. Accepting their failures opens up their minds to identifying their weaknesses and the areas in which they need to improve. Once they have identified those areas that need improvement, they can begin to put in the work to develop those areas of weakness. They consult with their coaches; they watch films and identify skills that they are good at or are lacking. Then they start hitting the gym to work on perfecting those skills.

The same idea is at work here in our Catholic faith. We examine our conscience, we go to Confession to confess our faults and to own up to our failings, and we humble ourselves to ask our merciful God for forgiveness and to bless us and to grant us His grace so that we can have the strength to overcome those weaknesses. As Catholics, the Sacrament of Penance is truly a gift from God that grants us the opportunity to bring to mind our sins and weaknesses and use that toward improvement and becoming better Christians. As Saint Augustine wrote, "The confession of evil works is the first beginning of good works." We wouldn't know what to improve on if we don't first humbly recognize our weaknesses.

According to the latest research in psychology about ethical behaviors, we have the tendency to repeat our failures because … we forget them easily.[66] Psychologists call this "ethical amnesia." When we commit acts that are unethical, we tend to want to forget them, and when we do try to remember them, the details become murky. That makes learning from our mistakes very difficult if we cannot accept our failings. If we cannot recognize our failings, we will not know what areas in our lives need improvement. Lack of self-awareness is one of the critical problems in leadership. In the business world, organizations spend a lot of time and effort looking for the problems and trying to fix them. They often look for areas that need fixing and areas that can use improvement; but often, when they look, they only look at the exteriors. They look for whatever external forces might have caused the problem. It is our natural inclination to want to be able to blame something else. We just don't spend as much time, nor do we choose, to look at the interior, at what is inside of the individual. We don't take as much time to self-reflect and correct our interior life. Leaders need to find the opportunity for self-reflection, and organizations need to grant them the time for such opportunities because it is important that leaders get to know themselves and examine their inner workings. Improvement often starts from within and extends to the outside—the organizations we run and the people we serve.

The Sacrament of Penance, if practiced wholeheartedly, gives us the opportunity to examine our conscience diligently and to recall even the smallest details of our indiscretions. Trying to bring our indiscretions to the surface of our memories will allow

---

[66] Kouchaki, M. and Gino, F. (2016). "Memories of unethical actions become obfuscated over time." *Proceedings of the National Academy of Sciences of the United States of America*. Vol.113, No.22.

us to learn from our mistakes and to remember to avoid repeating such actions that lead us to failure and to committing the sin. If we practice self-examination regularly, with true dedication, purity, and authenticity, we should be on our way to continuous growth toward spiritual perfection.

> *Three conditions are necessary for penance: contrition, which is sorrow for sin, together with a purpose of amendment; confession of sins without any omission; and satisfaction by means of good works.*
>
> *—Saint Thomas Aquinas*

PRAY AND ACT

*As the body without the spirit is dead,
so faith without deeds is dead.*

—*James 2:26*

Leadership Begins with Prayer

Leadership is an honorable and humbling task. Whosoever aspires to leadership desires a noble task (1 Timothy 3:1). That is why the practice of leadership must start on our knees, humbly in prayer. Saint Teresa of Avila said, "There are so many reasons why it is extremely important to begin with great determination in prayer." Just like the athletes and the musicians spending hours to practice their craft, leaders must also spend hours praying, in fact, to "pray without ceasing" (1 Thessalonians 5:17), to perfect their leadership craft. Leadership calls us to be perfect. And perfection is what we must strive for. "All the faithful, whatever their condition or state, are called by the Lord, each in his own way, to that perfect holiness whereby the Father Himself is perfect" (Lumen Gentium, Light to the Nations, 11). Leaders harken the way toward perfection. Perfection can be an intimidating call, and some have notably argued that we will never reach perfection. It does not mean, however, that we can just dismiss the gospel's call for us to be perfect (Matthew 5:48). We are all called to be perfect, just like our heavenly Father is perfect. Leaders can be imperfect, and we all are admittedly imperfect, but we must continuously strive to be perfect. The way toward perfection is not a walk in the park, but we have the saints to model after, for they too were admittedly imperfect but they did strive for perfection.

We can look to Saint Teresa of Avila, who makes the way of perfection accessible to us by teaching us in her book with that title. Prayer gives us the opportunity to reflect on our own strengths and weaknesses. According to Saint Teresa of Avila, we learn to know ourselves by endeavoring to know God through prayer. If we do not endeavor to know God, we may never know our true selves. By endeavoring to know God, we will learn what our abilities, our talents, and our purpose are. We will realize and acknowledge that they are all from God. Through prayer, we come to realize that everything we do as leaders is only possible because of God's grace.

Prayer humbles us and reminds us that our leadership efforts are for a much bigger and much higher purpose. Through prayer, we are reminded why we lead, and we come to understand the magnitude of our responsibilities. We are humbled as we are reminded of the opportunity that we have before us to serve God and to serve others as leaders. Prayer grants us the opportunity to realize our responsibility and be humbled, for it is in humility that we come to value others above ourselves. As leaders, we must value the interest of the people we lead and not our own self-interest (Philippians 2:3–4). We lead not for our own sake but for the sake of others. The call to lead is not a call to benefit ourselves, but a call to benefit those around us.

Prayer is a critical aspect of leadership. As we lead and guide others, we must begin on our knees. We must always remember to put Christ first and above all. Everything we do as leaders must stem from the love of Christ. We must continually seek guidance from God above. We pray so that God may grant us the strength to lead. We ask for guidance, wisdom, and strength from God to make our leadership good and effective. Without prayer, our leadership efforts would be fruitless. All of the leadership qualities and characteristics mentioned in this book—authenticity, humility, vision, courage, perseverance, persistence, grit—all have to be grounded in prayer. Prayer is like the glue that brings these characteristics together and holds them together, enabling leaders to lead soundly and effectively.

How to Begin the Day

In the Gospel of Mark, our Lord Jesus got up very early in the morning, while it was still dark, to go off to a solitary place to pray (Mark 1:35). That time of prayer was followed by preaching throughout Galilee, casting out demons, and healing the sick. Jesus shows us that no matter how long and busy our day will be, it is important that our daily activities start off with a prayer, even if it means waking up very early.

When I was discerning whether the religious life was my calling or not, part of the process was to explore come-and-see programs with several religious orders. Here I was given the opportunity not only to grow spiritually, but I also got to witness firsthand the dedication and devotion of some of our Church's seminarians and future leaders. I had the chance to pick up some habits from the religious groups that I now find very useful, even in secular life.

One habit that stuck with me is the habit of beginning every day early with prayer. Many of the religious orders that I stayed with would wake before the crack of dawn to get ready for their community morning prayers. Some individuals woke up even before the rest of the community got up so that they could spend time praying quietly on their own. It was such an amazing and awe-inspiring sight to see seminarians praying quietly in the early hours of the morning, drawing strength from God to carry them through the rest of their day.

I also got the privilege to witness different individual seminarian's daily routines. Some of them would work late into the night, studying and praying, and then still manage to wake up way before dawn. They just seemed so dedicated to expending all their energy to serving the Lord.

I was in the military for several years, so getting up super early in the morning is familiar to me, and I know being awake in the dreaded wee hours of the morning can make even the nicest people groggy, crabby, and grouchy. But when I lived with the different religious groups in their seminaries and novitiate houses, I was quite fascinated by what I observed. A busy daily routine, schoolwork, homework, plus service in the kitchen or whatever other duties can get anyone tired, sleep-deprived, and maybe even crabby in the early mornings, but not these seminarians and religious brothers. During my stay with them, I felt nothing but true joy circulating in the air, and it was the kind of joy that was just all around, spreading like wildfire in the seminary, even in the wee hours of the morning. The "good morning" greetings from the seminarians and the postulants came with a genuine smile. You could really feel their joy. They radiated the joy, and it was contagious. Whether the brothers were serving in the soup kitchen, cleaning their homes, serving at Mass, or studying Scripture, they amazingly stayed full of energy and joy. They were so joyful to do the work they were doing, no matter what that work was and no matter how early it was in the morning. I have never seen anything like it. They began each morning knowing what their purpose in life was. They invited Jesus into their lives early in the morning to be with them throughout the day. They woke up daily with a purpose. They knew exactly why they get out of bed in the morning. They knew their calling, and they were driven to fulfill it.

One early morning, I asked one of my roommates how he felt about waking up super early. He smiled and replied while we looked out the window of our bedroom, "Look outside. You see all those cars on the highway this early in the morning? Those are the people we have to serve." He paused for a few seconds and then quoted something in Latin that sounded like something he recites daily by heart: "*Servite Domino in laetitia!*"

I recognize some Latin words, but to be sure, I asked, "What does it mean?"

He went on to explain, "It is a quote from Saint Josemaria Escriva, founder of Opus Dei."

But before he could continue on explaining, I interrupted, "Opus Dei?" I had heard of the Latin phrase, but there were just too many Latin words for me to absorb that early in the morning.

But he seemed eager and happy with the opportunity to talk as if we were already in class. So he went further to explain, "The phrase *Opus Dei* is Latin for 'the work of God.' It is the name of an organization that teaches that everyone is called to holiness. The Latin phrase *Servite Domino in laetitia* translated to English is 'I will serve God joyfully!'"

I was truly appreciative of this informal lecture early in the morning, but I was mesmerized by his very sincere and enthusiastic delivery of his response. I was even more mesmerized by his explanation because it really did capture the actions and the sentiments that I observed during my time at that seminary. The seminarians there were some of the most devoted and dedicated group of individuals I have ever met. It also affirmed to me something else that I was wondering about Catholic vocations. I knew there that the future of our Church is in good hands. The devotion and the dedication that each seminarian had to their service to God, to God's Holy Church, and to their vocation, day in and day out, are exactly some of the leadership examples we need today.

> *Let go of your plans. The first hour of your morning belongs to God. Tackle the day's work that He charges you with, and He will give you the power to accomplish it.*
>
> —*Saint Teresa Benedicta*

Making Time for Prayer

In my time with the seminarians, I felt like I discovered their secret. It is not a well-kept secret, either, because it was easy to discover, and it was unfolding right before my eyes. The seminarians' secret to their energy, to their joy, and to their clear understanding of their calling in life is that they are fueled and inspired by prayer. Their days, no matter how busy, no matter how hectic, are structured by prayer. Each seminarian made sure that he had time for prayer. In between classes and service, they prayed. In between recreation and dinner, they prayed. No matter what day it was—whether it was a Monday, a Friday, or a Saturday—they started with prayer. Whether it was exam day or recreation day, they started with prayer. And it wasn't just allotted prayer time at the beginning or at the end of the day but all throughout the day.

Some of the religious groups I spent time with use the *Spiritual Exercises* that Saint Ignatius of Loyola shared with us. The *Spiritual Exercises* gives us a method that Saint Ignatius called *Examen* to help us structure and schedule our prayers. The *Examen* is a practice that the Jesuits today continue to do at least twice daily.

In our fast-paced and very busy modern lives, praying methodically twice a day is unheard of, but we can truly benefit from the Jesuits' five-step prayer structure. It is very difficult for many of us—especially those in the secular world, working nine to five, raising children, working a second job, and preparing dinner for the family—to find the time to pause and find a secluded place to pray. However, we must find the discipline to block off time and incorporate this much-needed prayer into our regular daily routine, not only because every religious person must do it but because we all need to pray.

It is hard to imagine anyone else busier than my good friends Gary and Anne. Gary and Anne are loving parents with five young kids. Both of them work full-time, and when they are not working, they are busy shuttling their kids from home to school to soccer practice and other extracurricular activities. And for some amazing reason, they have managed to prioritize and allot one hour every week to spend time with Jesus in the Blessed Sacrament at their local parish. Even as their family grew throughout the years, no matter how busy they got, they have stayed committed to their schedule of one holy hour a week for adoration.

Prayer is an important part of our daily routine. We all need prayer. Padre Pio said, "Prayer is the oxygen of the soul." As leaders, we need to pray to keep us focused toward our ultimate goal of fulfilling our vocations and to remind us of why we do what we do and why and how we lead. We need to pray to make sure that what we do is aligned with what God wills for us. We need to pray to keep us energized, motivated, and strengthened throughout our tiresome, busy days. We pray so that we draw our strength from God.

Saint Ignatius, in his rules, made sure that prayer was an integral part of his order's daily routine. This is how the Jesuits get the strength, inspiration, and joy to do the great things they do each day. Saint Ignatius thought that this technique was something that came from God and that he should share it as widely as possible. This is a method that leaders today can infuse into their daily lives to help them structure not only their busy days but to also structure their organizations, their mission, and the execution of their vision.

BJ Gonzalvo, Ph.D.

The Five-Step Method of the Daily *Examen* by Saint Ignatius of Loyola

Step 1: Stillness.

Find the time and the place to be alone with God so that you can be quiet and be still. A lot of us struggle with finding the time to be alone and quiet in this day and age. We are too busy, and we are afraid of being alone.

In a 2014 article published in *Science* magazine, participants of a study preferred to administer electric shock to themselves rather than sit alone in a room for twelve minutes.[67] Seventeenth-century scientist and philosopher Blaise Pascal wrote, "All of humanity's problems stem from man's inability to sit quietly in a room alone."

We have too many distractions and diversions nowadays, and so sitting alone in a quiet room is just not the ideal thing to do for many of us. But we need quiet time. We need to pause, pray, and recognize that being alone in the quiet is the chance for us to rejuvenate and gather strength and wisdom to carry out our tasks as leaders. Clear the mind. Be calm. Be still. Enter into the solitude of your heart where you can be alone with God. Carmelite friar, mystic, and Doctor of the Church, Saint John of the Cross, said, "It is best to learn to silence the faculties and to cause them to be still so that God may speak." Once we start to be still in our prayers, we begin to recognize that we are in the company of the Holy Spirit and know that the next minute or so is devoted solely to conversing with God. Slow down and let time stand still and know that God is in control. Be still and make your heart God's dwelling place.

---

[67] Timothy D. Wilson, David A. Reinhard, Eric C. Westgate, Daniel T. Gilbert, Nicole Ellerbeck, Cheryl Hahn, Casey L. Brown, Adi Shaked, "Just Think: The Challenges of the Disengaged Mind," *Science*, Vol.345, Issue 6192 (July 2014).

Step 2: Gratitude.

Review the day and give thanks for all the gifts and blessings. "Give thanks to the Lord for He is good and His love endures forever" (Psalm 118:1). Give thanks for the opportunity to lead, to inspire, and to draw others closer to God. Give thanks, for He has called you to lead. Showing gratitude is another lost art in this day and age. We seem to take for granted the many blessings that we receive daily. That attitude of gratitude is an often-forgotten but critical aspect of leadership. Leaders must be able to genuinely show their appreciation and respect for the role that they are in. Do not forget to express gratitude for the work people do to support you. Acknowledge the people around you and show them that what they do matters. Recognize them, and show them that you appreciate them. It's a phrase our lips utter a lot, but a simple and genuine "Thank you" can go a long way.

Great saintly leaders have a profound sense of gratitude. Do not forget to thank God for the blessings and for calling you to do His work and the opportunity to lead His people. Do not forget that the call to lead is not only a calling but a blessing.

Step 3: Reflection.

Reflect on the day and the different emotions that you felt that day. Are your internal feelings connected to your external actions? Are your talents connected to your core values? How did each situation affect your emotions? Did they facilitate your spiritual growth? Did the situations you were in bring you closer to God? Be aware of your own emotions as situations happen. Some can be detractors. Some situations can be stumbling blocks on your journey to holiness. Discern how God speaks to you in each of the situations.

Being aware of our current state is critical in reaching our future goal—the goal of being one with God. And as leaders, we need to constantly look inside ourselves. We need to stop blaming others and whatever external factors. We need to look inside and engage in a self-reflection exercise to bring things into focus as we do the work of God.

Step 4: Seek Forgiveness.

There are many challenges throughout the day, and we will have moments when we are far from being perfect. Leaders are far from being perfect. There are times when we go astray and we lead others astray. We must recall and recognize those moments and humbly ask for forgiveness. Ask for the strength to turn those moments of weakness into opportunities for growth so that you may have the opportunity to improve and better yourself. Even after a fault and failure, ask for forgiveness, and ask for the grace to be able to do better next time. It is not always easy to see our faults and admit our weaknesses, but these are the steps we need to take in order to get better and do better. God is a merciful and loving God, always ready to forgive us. We need to lower our pride and turn to God and admit our faults. Let us seek God's grace and embrace the forgiveness of God.

Step 5: Hopefulness.

Padre Pio once said, "Pray, hope, and don't worry." Trust in God's grace and mercy that He grant us another opportunity and that we take that opportunity to grow in spirit. Ask God for strength and wisdom as you continue on your journey as a leader. May the God of hope fill you with joy and peace as you trust in Him, so that you may overflow with hope. Stock up on hope so that you can turn around and share that hope with the people you lead. There will be times of hopelessness and despair, but you, as a leader, will have to remember that you are the purveyor of hope. Be the leader to inspire hope in others.

> *True and certain is that hope which is accompanied by good works. But if it goes alone, it ought to be called presumption.*
>
> —Saint Lawrence Justinian

Practice to Perfect Your Prayer

For nurturing the interior life, for more on how to grow in our prayers, and for how to have a deep and intimate conversation with God, let us look to the examples of Saint Teresa of Avila, a mystic and a Doctor of the Church. Through her writings in *The Way of Perfection* and *The Interior Castle*, we get a practical guide for how to progress through prayer and how to live a spiritual life that is in union with God. Because, yes, our prayer life can get better. There is always room for improvement when it comes to our prayer life. Saint Teresa points out that growth in our prayer means growth in our holiness.

Everyone is called to pray, especially those who lead others. And it is a call not just to pray aloud but to pray quietly, in the silence of our hearts and mind. According to Saint John of the Cross, "What we need most in order to make progress is to be silent before this great God with our appetite and with our tongue, for the language He best hears is silent love." Leaders are often expected to be vocal and are often surrounded by people, but it is very important that leaders find the time and the space to be silent and to have that quiet dialogue with God. Saint Augustine, Saint John Chrysostom, Saint Jerome, Saint Bernard of Clairvaux, Saint Teresa of Avila, and Mother Teresa have all recommended quiet and mental prayer and the need to meditate on God's words and contemplate God's love. According to Saint Alphonsus Liguori, "All saints have become saints by mental prayer." We must practice mental prayer. We must learn to place ourselves in God's presence and contemplate that God longs to be with us, in our hearts and in our minds. The saints recognized that meditating does not come easily, and yet, they did it. Padre Pio taught us: "Have patience and persevere in the holy exercise of meditation; be content to begin with small steps until you have legs to run, better still, wings to fly." Start with one small prayer, and slowly but surely, strive to make progress toward perfecting your prayer.

> *If only world leaders could enter this exalted consciousness. It would be so much more worthwhile for them to strive for this state of prayer than for all the power in the world.*
>
> —Saint Teresa of Avila, *The Book of My Life*

Prayer Happens

Praying is an act of love according to Saint Teresa of Avila. It is a conversation between you and God. And it does not have to be done only inside a church building. It doesn't only have to happen when we are on our knees or with hands clasped together with our heads bowed down. It is important to have those kinds of formal and traditional prayers, but prayer should be done incessantly (see 1 Thessalonians 5:17). Prayer can be done virtually anywhere; for wherever we are, God is. Whatever it is we do, we must continue to seek God. As Saint Bonaventure said, "In everything, whether it is a thing sensed or a thing known, God Himself is hidden within."

Saint John Bosco thought that praying is speaking with God in the kitchen or while seated on the grass, gazing at the heavens.

Brother Lawrence, author of the spiritual classic, *Practice of the Presence of God*, prayed and found God while washing the dishes. He found God amongst the pots and pans. It was Brother

Lawrence who also thought that it is a great delusion for prayer time to be different from other times. Prayer and invoking the presence of God can and should happen anywhere, even in the most mundane of all activities.

Saint Josemaria Escriva, for instance, experienced what he later described as his "most elevated prayer" on a busy street in Madrid. One day, he was trying to pray inside the quiet church, but he wasn't having much success at it, so he stepped out of the church, walked the busy streets of Madrid, and got on a streetcar. And it was there in that busy streetcar where he experienced a period of sublime prayer where he was lost in contemplation of the marvelous reality that God is our Father. Who knew that what he called his most elevated prayer would come during a streetcar ride?! That profound realization hit him so hard, his heart and lips were moved to exclaim, "*Abba, Pater!*"

Prayer Plus Action

We may speak with Jesus as we walk by the way, and he says, I am at thy right hand. We may commune with God in our hearts, we may walk in companionship with Christ. When engaged in our daily labor, we may breathe out our heart's desire, inaudible to any human ear; but that word cannot die away into silence, nor can it be lost. Nothing can drown the soul's desire. It rises above the din of the street, above the noise of machinery. It is God to whom we are speaking, and our prayer is heard.

—Brother Lawrence, *Practice of the Presence of God*

Just as it says in the Epistle of James, what good is faith without works?[68] Our prayer without action is worthless. Some of our best moments come after we have prayed, and the saints can attest to this. After spending time in solitude and prayer, and after discerning the will of God in their lives, the saints were empowered to step up to carry out God's will into the world. They did not wait for the next person to step up and lead. Mother Teresa said, "Do not wait for leaders; do it alone, person to person." Prayer can empower us to get inspired and motivated to act. We can try to seek out God's will some more in quiet prayer and in solitude, but as leaders, we are called to action, and we have to carry out the work that we are called to do. Prayer doesn't necessarily have to stop, but instead, prayer becomes one with the action. It is in carrying out that work will we hear God's guiding voice.

> *I sought to hear the voice of God and climbed the topmost steeple. But God declared: Go down again–I dwell among the people.*
>
> —Cardinal John Henry Newman

As a church leader, Cardinal Newman realized that God's people were not hanging out on the topmost steeple. God's people were down below. He needed to get down to be in touch with the people he served. With the people is where leaders will see God. With the people is where leaders will hear God's voice and where leaders will know what God is calling them to do. Mother Teresa used to say that each one of the poor she served was "Jesus in disguise."

Our leadership starts now, with the very next person we will encounter. Let us treat that person as Mother Teresa treated every

---

[68] see James 2:14

person she met—like that person was Jesus. Let us treat that person with respect, honor, and dignity, as a child of God, made in the Divine image. That person might be your child, or your teacher, maybe even your boss at work or your least-liked coworker. The opportunity for us to be leaders is right there and then. It is our calling, and we need to open our hearts and ears to hear it. Let us accept that call to lead with love so that we, ourselves, will lead with love. "Love must be sincere" (Romans 12:9). Leading with love is a lost art and it might not sound like a professional attribute for leaders to have, but love should be an integral part of our leadership. We should not be ashamed to lead with love. Let us remember what Saint Paul told us in his letter to the Corinthians (13:4–8):

> Love is patient. Love is kind.
> It does not dishonor others, it is not
> self-seeking, it is not easily angered,
> it keeps no record of wrongs.
> Love does not delight in evil but
> rejoices with the truth.
> It always protects, always trusts,
> always hopes, always perseveres.
> Love never fails.

Joyful Response to the Call

Let us respond to the call to lead and the call to be saints with joy and courage. Saint Katharine Drexel was a missionary nun serving minorities in the United States during the 1940s and 1950s. This period was a challenging time to be serving minorities in America. She was harassed many times by segregationists, and they even had one of her schools burned down. But she did not despair. She did not give up. Instead, she pressed on with joy and courage. As a well-off child from a rich family in Philadelphia, she really did not have to do any of the work she was doing. She did not have to deal with any of the hardships that she encountered. She could have been something else in life other than a hardworking nun. She had enough wealth, and she did not have to do any of the service to the poor and the forgotten. Instead, she stood up with courage to answer God's calling and to go where she was needed. She gave up her wealth, founded a religious order dedicated to serving Native Americans and African Americans, and funded the setting up of a system of over sixty Catholic schools and mission centers throughout the United States.

> *If we wish to serve God and love our neighbor well, we must manifest our joy in the service we render to Him and them. Let us open wide our hearts. It is joy which invites us. Press forward and fear nothing.*
>
> —Katharine Drexel

Leading in the Moment

Great leaders do the work where the greatest needs are. Leaders act not based on what they want to do; they act because they realize that there is a need. Mother Teresa saw the needs of the poor in the streets of Calcutta, and she stepped up to do something about it. Saint Francis saw the Church was in ruins, and he stepped up and started to personally do the rebuilding.

Saint John Bosco saw a poor child living in the streets, and so he stepped up and took him in and educated him.

The saints started small, but it was their dedication to their calling that fueled the growth of their leadership and eventually the growth of their organization. It was their love for God and for their fellow human beings that drove them to act and to lead. They were responding to the call of the moment, and so they led in the moment. They embraced the call of the moment.

> *You know well enough that Our Lord does not look so much at the greatness of our actions, nor even at their difficulty, but at the love with which we do them.*
>
> *—Saint Therese of Lisieux*

We do not have to be the founding leaders of the next great institution, like Saints Francis, Dominic, Ignatius, or Mother Teresa. Actually, the saints were not intending to found organizations when they started doing their work. They were simply and humbly doing what they could to make the lives of people around them better and doing their best to do the will of God. Their leadership emerged as a result of their response in the moment. They did not envision moving mountains. Their vision was not ambitious at all. They simply responded to the needs of each person they encountered in that moment. They did not go out seeking greatness for themselves for they knew that the earthly idea of greatness is illusory. But instead, in their striving for holiness and doing the will of God to the best of their abilities, one holy act at a time, greatness found them.

> *Our Christian destiny is, in fact, a great one: but we cannot achieve greatness unless we lose all interest in being great.*
>
> —Thomas Merton, No Man is an Island

That call to be a saint is ours. Let us embrace that call. And within that call is the call to lead—the call to lead our brothers and sisters, to ignite them, guide them, and empower them. Going back to what John C. Maxwell said about leaders: "A leader is one who knows the way, goes the way, and shows the way." And so as Christians, our Lord has shown us that way, and so we should know that way. We must go that way. And we must show others that way.

A Leadership Model for Each One of Us

There is great diversity in the leadership styles of the saints. We are blessed to have all kinds of saints. And that is great for those of us who are striving to be like the saints because there is likely to be a leadership style for each and every one of us to model after. There's the quiet and contemplative style we can find in Saint Therese of Lisieux and Saint Faustina. There's the outspokenness of Saint Catherine of Siena and Saint Paul. There's the military-oriented leadership of Saint Joan of Arc and Saint Ignatius. There's the outgoing and energetic leadership of Saint Teresa of Avila and Saint Francis Xavier. There's the hardworking hands-on leadership style of Mother Theresa. There's the intelligent and philosophical style of Saint Thomas Aquinas and Saint Augustine.

We all have our own list of favorite saints. I know I have my own personal list, and it's a growing one, especially as I continue to learn more about the other saints. The saints I highlight in this book are mostly the saints that I am familiar with at the moment, and I am sure that there are more saints that I have yet to encounter. Their lives and stories of leadership motivate and inspire me and countless others. And depending on the situation or the kind of work that needs to be done, there is a saint for every occasion and for every person. The work of the Lord is rich in diversity, and there is a great diversity among the workers in the vineyard of the Lord. So I encourage you to take the time to explore the lives of the saints and find the ones who you would like to model after. I'm sure that you will find one or two or three or more. In our Lord's vineyard, there is a lot of work that needs to be done, but remember that, as Saint Catherine of Siena said, "You are rewarded not according to your work or your time, but according to the measure of your love."

Hope to Inspire

I hope you find this book worthwhile and helpful. I hope that I was able to introduce or reintroduce to you the saints, who can help show us the way as well as show us how to lead and show others the way. I hope the examples of the saints provide you, the reader, with some of the most inspirational leadership examples. But just know that we are barely scratching the surface here. In this journey of discovery, I was able to cover only a small fraction of what the lives of the saints have to offer. There are many other nuggets of wisdom that we can discover, but remember that we have to pursue that treasure and spend the time to get to know the saints more. And I fervently urge you to thoroughly explore their lives and their stories. Have your own journey of discovery. Discover, or perhaps rediscover, how full of wisdom the lives of the saints are. "The saints are our friends," as Father Benedict Groeschel used to say. They are our friends who are now looking down upon us, praying for us, and guiding us. Our older brothers and sisters in heaven want nothing but the best for us.

I hope their examples move you, enrich your spiritual life, and inspire you. I used the word *inspire* quite frequently in this book, not only because many of the saints I described are truly inspirational but because to inspire is a key aspect of leadership. Great leaders inspire. The word *inspire* comes from the Latin word *inspirare*, which means "to breathe life into" or "to blow into." Leaders breathe life into their followers, into their organizations, and into the mission and vision of their organizations. The word *spirit* also comes from the same root word. And thus, as leaders inspire, their spirit is transmitted as well.

Such metaphysical characterization of leadership, especially in secular circles, is rare and we seem to have forgotten the roots of leadership. But to inspire, to breathe life into what we do as leaders is what true leadership is about. The inspiration Mother Teresa left two decades ago is still with the Missionaries of Charity as they continue to serve the poor around the world. The inspiration that Saint John Bosco started over a hundred years ago is still with us today in the Salesians, who continue to evangelize and educate the young people around the world. The inspiration that Saint Francis of Assisi started over eight hundred years ago is again very vibrant today as we have Pope Francis using that same *spirit* to *inspire* our generation. Their leadership was so profound and so powerful that it continues to be with us in spirit, inspiring us to love and to serve and to lead.

Praise for Spiritual Blessings in Christ (Ephesians 1:3–23)

Praise be to the God and Father of our Lord Jesus Christ, who has blessed us in the heavenly realms with every spiritual blessing in Christ. For He chose us in Him before the creation of the world to be holy and blameless in His sight.

In love He predestined us for adoption to sonship through Jesus Christ, in accordance with His pleasure and will— to the praise of His glorious grace, which He has freely given us in the One He loves.

In Him we have redemption through His blood, the forgiveness of sins, in accordance with the riches of God's grace that He lavished on us. With all wisdom and understanding, He made known to us the mystery of His will according to His good pleasure, which He purposed in Christ, to be put into effect when the times reach their fulfillment—to bring unity to all things in heaven and on earth under Christ.

In Him we were also chosen, having been predestined according to the plan of Him who works out everything in conformity with the purpose of His will, in order that we, who were the first to put our hope in Christ, might be for the praise of His glory. And you also were included in Christ when you heard the message of truth, the gospel of your salvation. When you believed, you were marked in Him with a seal, the promised

Holy Spirit, who is a deposit guaranteeing our inheritance until the redemption of those who are God's possession—to the praise of His glory.

Thanksgiving and Prayer

For this reason, ever since I heard about your faith in the Lord Jesus and your love for all God's people, I have not stopped giving thanks for you, remembering you in my prayers. I keep asking that the God of our Lord Jesus Christ, the glorious Father, may give you the Spirit of wisdom and revelation, so that you may know Him better.

I pray that the eyes of your heart may be enlightened in order that you may know the hope to which He has called you, the riches of His glorious inheritance in His holy people, and His incomparably great power for us who believe. That power is the same as the mighty strength He exerted when He raised Christ from the dead and seated Him at His right hand in the heavenly realms, far above all rule and authority, power and dominion, and every name that is invoked, not only in the present age but also in the one to come. And God placed all things under His feet and appointed Him to be head over everything for the church, which is His body, the fullness of Him who fills everything in every way.

SUGGESTIONS FOR FURTHER READINGS

As you decide to respond to the call to holiness and the call to lead, there is a wealth of wisdom in the books by the saints and about the saints that I'd be more than happy to recommend for your journey. The call to lead is, first and foremost, a call to holiness. It would be impossible to lead others if we cannot even lead ourselves. "If the blind lead the blind, both will fall into the pit" (Matthew 15:14). So the first step to becoming an effective leader is to first lead yourself to respond to the call to holiness. Just like the saints, before they were able to lead others, they first strengthened their own spirituality. And if you're looking for some examples and inspiration for how to strengthen your spirituality, what better place to look than the lives of the saints themselves, who share with us their stories and their prayers? There are many entry points to learning more about the spiritual lives of the saints that could guide you to the path to holiness. Reading autobiographical accounts of their lives is one great starting point, and that is what I would highly recommend. In their autobiographies, you get a glimpse into their interior life, their thoughts, and their mental prayers. Below is a list of wonderful books and writings by the saints and about the saints to guide you on your journey. And I hope that you will find it helpful.

BJ Gonzalvo, Ph.D.

Confessions by Saint Augustine

One enlightening entry point into the spiritual life is Saint Augustine's *Confessions*. Saint Augustine, Bishop of Hippo—which is now modern-day Annaba, Algeria—wrote this book himself in the late fourth century. Reading this book marks a very pivotal moment in my life and also, as I hear, in the lives of many others. This book was the first spiritual book I ever read, and the very first book that I read as a young adult since high school. I first picked up this book when I was in my early twenties at this big-box store with a coffee shop. Sipping a hot cup of coffee in one of those bookstores was the hip thing to do during that time, and as a young adult, I found this to be a very relaxing, very mature kind of thing to do. I was not much into reading before, but as I browsed around this big-box bookstore, I saw this book with this catchy one-word title written on a black, blank hardcover: *Confessions*. I had heard the name Saint Augustine, but I really had no idea who he was. The title of the book got me curious, so I picked it up. I started to read the first lines as I stood in front of the shelf; and then several pages into it, I had to grab a seat so I could sit down. I just knew that I was going to be reading for a while. I could not put the book down. I got some coffee, sat down, and read some more. I was not able to finish reading the book in the bookstore, so I ended up purchasing it so I could take it home and read later. It was a book that turned my life into a whole new direction. It was a book that opened my heart and my mind in so many ways. I wasn't much of a reader then, but I also wasn't that much of a spiritual or religious person either. Something about that book transformed me in so many ways.

Saint Augustine's story, even though it's from the fourth century, is a story that many of us can relate to, even this day and age. Saint Augustine wrote about his struggles as a young adult. Just like me and many other young adults today, he got off to a start in life that put him at odds with God's will. He encountered all kinds of temptations—greed, heresy, promiscuity, etc. And he often fell into sin. He felt restless, with no firm direction in life. His mother, Saint Monica, could not do much to intervene except to pray for him. And yes, she prayed. She prayed incessantly, fervently, and relentlessly for her son's waywardness and conversion to God. She was steadfast in her prayers and did not lose hope. It took years of praying, fasting, and weeping on her son's behalf, but God heard her prayers. In God's time, Augustine, eventually, was graced to find that spiritual door back to God. After years of exploring, getting lost, and falling down, he would finally be found and be back on the right path. His is a path that is familiar to many of us Christians. We all have our struggles in life where we fall down, but with the grace of God, we get back up on our feet to soldier on. There's a lot we can learn from Saint Augustine and Saint Monica. I know that I always have my mother praying for me and making sure that I'm doing the will of God.

Saint Augustine's philosophical insights and wisdom are timeless. Something about his writings undeniably gets to the heart of the very essence of our humanity and our relationship with God. The ways he explored and discussed his inner conflicts, his memory of his childhood, his unconscious desires, his dreams, the relationship between his mind and his body—these are universal psychological and spiritual experiences that we all can relate to. He was a bishop, a Church leader. His writings and wisdom on leadership are underutilized, but we can certainly learn a great deal from his leadership principles.

Here are some well-known quotes by Saint Augustine about leadership (from Saint Augustine's Sermon on Pastors):

> *The first aspect is that I am a Christian; the second, that I am a leader. I am a Christian for my own sake, whereas I am a leader for your sake; the fact that I am a Christian is to my own advantage, but I am a leader for your advantage.*

> *Do you wish to rise? Begin by descending.*
> *You plan a tower that will pierce the clouds?*
> *Lay first the foundation of humility.*
> *No man can be a good bishop if he*
> *loves his title but not his task.*

I highly recommend that the book *Confessions* be at the top of your must-read list. Reading this book is the opportunity for us to converse and get to know, even befriend, Saint Augustine. Let's ask him how to go about finding God. Let's ask him how to go about leading others. And as you converse with him in your reading, add this prayer.

> *O holy Saint Augustine, who has*
> *famously declared that*
> *"Our hearts were made for You, O Lord, and*
> *they are restless until they rest in You."*
> *Aid me in my own search for our Lord*
> *that through your intercession*
> *I may be granted the wisdom to determine*
> *the purpose God has planned for me.*
> *Pray that I be blessed with the*
> *courage to follow God's will*
> *even at times when I do not understand.*
> *Ask our Lord to lead me to a*
> *life worthy of His love,*
> *that I may one day share the*
> *riches of His kingdom.*
> *Petition our Lord and Savior to ease*
> *the burden of my problems*
> *and grant my special intention,*
> *and I will honor you all of my days.*

The Autobiography of Saint Therese of Lisieux: The Story of a Soul

This book is a spiritual classic that is a must-read for anyone who wants to get on this spiritual quest to know God on a deeper level. Saint Therese wrote this book two years before her death in 1897. She went home to God at the young age of twenty-four. Other than her family and her sisters in the convent, no one really knew Saint Therese. A year after she died, her book was printed with the intention of sharing it only with the Carmelite convents and her family. Other people found the book, and requests kept coming in for copies. The book quickly became a hit. In today's language, it went *viral*. In fact, it continues to be a publishing wonder even today as it influences so many people. Talk about quiet leadership. She leads us even more now that she is dead than when she was alive. Saint Therese never left the convent to travel or to go on missions. And she had always wanted to go on missions. But for some reason, she knew that her mission, which was to make God loved, would begin after her death. On her deathbed, she vowed, "I will spend my heaven doing good on earth. I will let fall a shower of roses." Now her book and her relic travel around the world, inspiring, evangelizing, and converting people. She draws us into her prayer because that is her pledge to us—to spend her time in heaven doing good on earth. And the roses are her signature, signaling to us that she is listening to our prayers.

We know her as "The Little Flower," for she was a small and simple flower of God. We also know her as "Saint Therese of the Child Jesus." She had a childlike simplicity and faith in God. We also know her for her "little way," for she saw herself as small and humble, and she did ordinary things with extraordinary love. She prayed like a child, with complete confidence in God's love and complete obedience to His will.

For anyone wanting to advance in their quest to get to know the love of God, pick up this book and learn Saint Therese's ways.

Her autobiography is a great resource for leaders. Leaders tend to be externally focused and always in the eye of the public. They are always looking out for their people. Leaders rarely get a chance to have that quiet interior life. Here, in this book, is a leader's chance to venture inward, slow down the pace, read, and listen to the quiet love of Saint Therese for God.

Get to know Saint Therese; befriend her and follow her humble little way to God. Leaders can use such humility. Below is a Novena to Saint Therese that we can all make as we seek to get to know her and befriend her.

The Novena Rose Prayer

O Little Therese of the Child Jesus, please pick for me a rose from the heavenly gardens and send it to me as a message of love. O Little Flower of Jesus, ask God to grant the favors I now place with confidence in your hands ...

[mention your intention in silence here]

Saint Therese, help me to always believe as you did in God's great love for me, so that I might imitate your "Little Way" each day. Amen.

The Autobiography by Saint Teresa of Avila

Here is another classic that has influenced so many other saints, such as Saint Therese of Lisieux, Saint Teresa Benedicta of the Cross, Mother Teresa, and many others, especially those who took the name "Teresa." Talk about having an interior life—her writings, which include *The Autobiography, The Interior Castle,* and *The Way of Perfection,* are very important books to have in your library as you go out on the quest for advancing in your spiritual life. Saint Teresa Benedicta, also known as Edith Stein, upon reading Saint Teresa's autobiography, immediately put down the book and exclaimed to herself, "This is the truth." That reading was an important instance in Saint Teresa Benedicta's life as it is a significant marker of the period of her conversion. We too can have one of Saint Teresa's books as markers of our conversion. It does not have to be similar to the conversion that Edith Stein went through, but it can be a daily conversion back to the path of holiness. Conversion does not have to be a one-time event. It can be moments of conversion where we feel ourselves go adrift but then we course-correct and get back on the right track. When you read Saint Teresa's conversations with God, you will sense that we too can have similar conversations with God—just like how we converse with our friends.

Prayer of Saint Teresa of Avila
Let nothing disturb you, Let nothing frighten you,
All things are passing away; God never changes.
Patience obtains all things. Whoever
has God lacks nothing;
God alone suffices.

The Autobiography of Saint Ignatius of Loyola

Some of the most important contributions to Christian spirituality came from Saint Ignatius of Loyola. From him, not only do we get the Society of Jesus—better known as the Jesuits—but we also get one of the greatest spiritual classics, the *Spiritual Exercises*—a compilation of meditations, prayers, and contemplative practices. It is a book that has profoundly influenced many spiritual seekers over the centuries and has helped many people deepen their relationship with God. And if we want to have an intimate understanding of this spiritual classic and its author, this autobiography is a must-read. This book gives us an insight into his spiritual life, his inspirations, and his thoughts. He was a man on a mission with a vision of doing great things, all for the greater glory of God—*Ad Majorem Dei Gloriam.*

Suscipe
Take, Lord, and receive all my liberty, my memory, my understanding and my entire will, All I have and call my own. You have given all to me. To You, Lord, I return it. Everything is Yours; do with it what You will. Give me only Your love and Your grace. That is enough for me.

—Spiritual Exercises #234

Saint Francis of Assisi

Not too many of the saints got to write an autobiography. In fact, not a lot of the saints got to write anything at all, and all we know about them is through second-hand accounts of their lives and their deeds. Saint Francis is one of the most popular and most beloved saints, and yet we do not have anything written by him. A lot of the things we know about him are through secondary accounts of his friars, historians, and people who knew him. Some of the best resources about Saint Francis come from biographers who wrote about the details of his life, like G. K. Chesterton and Saint Bonaventure.

The Life of Saint Francis of Assisi by **Saint Bonaventure**.

We owe a great deal of gratitude to Saint Bonaventure for the insights he gives us into Saint Francis of Assisi from the eyewitness accounts contained in his writings. He was born in 1218, became a friar in 1243, and died in 1274, a mere fifty years after the death of Saint Francis in 1226. He became the minister general of the order when he was forty years old. He was a theologian, a teacher of the faith, and was regarded as one of the greatest philosophers of the Middle Ages. He was also a friend of the great theologian and Doctor of the Church, Saint Thomas Aquinas. Saint Bonaventure was made a Cardinal and, in 1588, he was declared a Doctor of the Church. He also wrote another book called *The Mind's Journey to God*—another book to add to our spiritual bookshelves that is bound to stimulate both intellectually and spiritually.

In his book about the life of Saint Francis, we have a saint writing about another saint. His presence during the early years of the Franciscan order enabled him to reveal to us the reality of the lives of the Mendicant Order. Not only does he present a biographical work that opens up a window for us all into the world of Saint Francis, but his writing also leads us on a path that we can follow, the same path that shows us how Francis loved and imitated our Lord Jesus Christ.

***

Prayer of Saint Bonaventure
Pierce, O most sweet Lord Jesus, my inmost soul with the most joyous and healthful wound of Thy love, and with true, calm and most holy apostolic charity, that my soul may ever languish and melt with entire love and longing for Thee, may yearn for Thee and for Thy courts, may long to be dissolved and to be with Thee. Grant that my soul may hunger after Thee, the Bread of Angels, the refreshment of holy souls,

our daily and supersubstantial bread, having all sweetness and savor and every delightful taste. May my heart ever hunger after and feed upon Thee, Whom the angels desire to look upon, and may my inmost soul be filled with the sweetness of Thy savor; may it ever thirst for Thee, the fountain of life, the fountain of wisdom and knowledge, the fountain of eternal light, the torrent of pleasure, the fullness of the house of God; may it ever compass Thee, seek Thee, find Thee, run to Thee, come up to Thee, meditate on Thee, speak of Thee, and do all for the praise and glory of Thy name, with humility and discretion, with love and delight, with ease and affection, with perseverance to the end; and be Thou alone ever my hope, my entire confidence, my riches, my delight, my pleasure, my joy, my rest and tranquility, my peace, my sweetness, my food, my refreshment, my refuge, my help, my wisdom, my portion, my possession, my treasure; in Whom may my mind and my heart be ever fixed and firm and rooted immovably.
Amen.

Saint Francis of Assisi by G. K. Chesterton

G. K. Chesterton published this biographical work about the life of Saint Francis shortly after his conversion to Roman Catholicism. Reading this book is a great way for us living in modern times to get introduced to our beloved Saint Francis, who lived over eight hundred years ago.

> *The Christian ideal has not been*
> *tried and found wanting.*
> *It has been found difficult; and left untried.*
>
> —G. K. Chesterton

Joan of Arc

There are many biographical and historical books about Saint Joan of Arc. One in particular by Kelly DeVries, *Joan of Arc: A Military Leader*, takes an in-depth look at her incredible military leadership, aptitude, and how she was able to use what she had envisioned through Divine providence to guide her in her leadership such that her soldiers trusted and followed her.

> *One life is all we have and we live it as we believe in living it. But to sacrifice what you are and to live without belief, that is a fate more terrible than dying.*
>
> —Saint Joan of Arc

Practice in the Presence of God: The Wisdom and Teachings of Brother Lawrence

As the book title alone implies, we are called to practice living our daily lives in the presence of God. As Christians striving for holiness, we must always develop the practice of being aware of the presence of God in our lives. This book is a classic and a must-read, not just for those living in religious communities but also those living in contemporary secular settings who seek God and meaning in even the most mundane tasks. Brother Lawrence, a humble cook and dishwasher, discovered that God is present in the most ordinary things, even in the pots and pans. Brother Lawrence, through his writings and his companionship, helps us find God in our own daily practices as we live out our own callings in life to the fullest.

> *That all things are possible to him who believes, that they are less difficult to him who hopes, they are more easy to him who loves, and still more easy to him who perseveres in the practice of these three virtues.*
>
> *—Brother Lawrence*

DEDICATION

To my wife, Jennifer, for your steadfast support and encouragement, and your selfless and unconditional love.

To my children, Adelynn, Blaise, and Dominic, my source of joy, strength, and inspiration.

To my parents, Benjamin and Veronica, for teaching me how to pray and for leading us, your children, to know God and His love. And to my brother, EJ, for showing me true and fun brotherly love!

ACKNOWLEDGMENTS

A book is a reflection of the people around us and of those who have influenced us. I have encountered many leaders in my life, those with titles and those who don't even know that they are leaders, who have influenced me in profound ways.

To all those who have given me support and guidance, not only during the actual writing of this book, but throughout my entire life, THANK YOU. Thank you for the inspiration, the motivation, and for standing by me.

To Father Dan and Father Ray, for your leadership and mentorship, thank you.

To the Couples for Christ – Foundation for Family and Life (CFC-FFL), most especially my household group, thank you for the fun-filled, Christ-centered friendships.

To my editor, Dennis McGeehan, for your steady guidance, grace, and brilliance, thank you.

To the seminarians at Divine Word College in Epworth and to the brothers and sisters of the Franciscan Friars of the Renewal in New York—thank you for your prayers, your insights and inspiration.

To Father Benedict Joseph Groeschel, I never got the chance to tell you but you have influenced me in so many ways. Please continue praying for us.

SAINTLY-NEST.COM

The Wisdom of the Saints for Our Modern Lives

CPSIA information can be obtained
at www.ICGtesting.com
Printed in the USA
FSOW01n0351260717
36709FS